THE 10 COMMANDMENTS OF
marriage

THE 10 COMMANDMENTS OF
marriage

The Dos and Don'ts for a Lifelong Covenant

ED YOUNG

MOODY PUBLISHERS
CHICAGO

All Scripture quotations, unless otherwise indicated, are taken from the *New American Standard Bible*®, Copyright © The Lockman Foundation 1960, 1962, 1963, 1968, 1971, 1972, 1973, 1975, 1977, 1995. Used by permission.

Scripture quotations marked NIV are taken from the *Holy Bible, New International Version*®. NIV®. Copyright © 1973, 1978, 1984 by International Bible Society. Used by permission of Zondervan Publishing House. All rights reserved.

Scripture quotations marked KJV are taken from the King James Version.

Library of Congress Cataloging-in-Publication Data

Young, Ed, 1961-
    The 10 commandments of marriage : dos and don'ts for a lifelong covenant /
Ed Young.
        p. cm.
    Includes bibliographical references.
    ISBN 0-8024-3146-1
    1. Marriage--Religious aspects--Christianity. I. Title: Ten commandments of marriage. II. Title.

BV835.Y67 2003
248.8'44--dc21

2003000355

3 5 7 9 10 8 6 4 2

Printed in the United States of America

To my covenant partner, Jo Beth.
You are the love of my life!

Also to my three sons and their covenant partners:
Ed and Lisa, Ben and Elliott, Cliff and Danielle

And to my seven granddaughters,
LeeBeth, Laurie, Landra, Nicole, Claire, Rachel, and Susannah;
And to my grandson, E. J.

CONTENTS

Yes, Keith and I have been spiritually motivated and moved in the time we've spent with them, but we've also laughed our heads off. *Without compromise.* That's the kind of company I like.

I could tell you lots of wonderful things about the Youngs; things I've noted from a distance and things I've witnessed up close. Perhaps the most pertinent in terms of the book you are holding is that they have a great marriage. You won't make it through the appetizer sitting across the restaurant table from them before you clearly see that Ed and Jo Beth Young are crazy about each other.

They have undoubtedly done something that worked. *The 10 Commandments of Marriage* not only tells you what, it tells you how. They took the principles of Scripture and had the courage to test them on the linoleum glued to average life on planet Earth. The Word worked. God worked. And make no mistake about it, the Youngs worked.

God has blessed this Houston-resident shepherd with a flock bulging over the fence. Yes, I'm impressed with those numbers because I know the doctrine is sound but I am far more impressed with his personal set of statistics: sons, daughters-in-law, and grandchildren who have also been swept off their feet by the love of God and planted in pastures where numbers flock to hear their messages of Truth, whether spoken or sung. Dr. Young and I and every other person who dares to write a book must ask ourselves a vital question: would our families "buy" it? Believe it? Confirm it?

Dr. Ed Young's family buys it. So does this friend. You can, too. But don't just buy it. Receive it. Test the biblical principles for yourself. Give God a little time and cooperation and your kids will buy it, too. God transforms families. Take it from one who knows firsthand. He can pull any life out of a pit and use one devoted heart to transform an entire family line. *You* be the one.

I'm so glad the fence is down. This is a shepherd sheep can trust.

BETH MOORE

FOREWORD

One sure way to know if God desires to enlarge a shepherd's borders (1 Chronicles 4:10) is a fence bulging and breaking from the overcrowding of the present flock. I have the privilege of residing and serving in the same city with Pastor Ed Young. I can testify firsthand that the flock God has entrusted to him has undoubtedly multipled until the fence of his ministry's former perimeters—albeit wide by anyone's standards—is down. A second location in Houston has proved helpful to meet the needs of growing crowds but as soon as the new pasture opened, the flock once again outgrew the fence.

The draw? The work of God through the smart, witty, and relevant pulpit teaching of Dr. Young. It's simply time the man wrote another book and offered a much bigger flock a little breathing room.

I also know Jo Beth Young, his wife. Call me picky, but I buy a message much quicker when it is propped up by the real thing behind the billboard. I like a public persona that's not a misfit to its private side. This man and his message *fit*. My husband, Keith, and I have had the pleasure of getting to know Dr. and Mrs. Young personally. They both captured my heart when they were more taken with my husband than with his wife. We not only have a great respect for the Youngs—*we like them.*

PREFACE

At a national conference for the American Association for Marital and Family Therapy, Dr. Mark Carpol shared one question that he believes is at the heart of all marriage counseling. He contends that couples that honestly consider and answer this question throughout their married lives would rarely, if ever, need marital therapy. The question he encouraged every husband to ask himself and every wife to ask herself is, "What is it like being married to me?"

That is a great question! By no means is it a cure-all to marital problems, but it's a super tool for helping couples think of ways they can enhance their marriages and deepen their intimacy. I believe that if every husband and wife were to ask themselves that question and be *totally honest* in their answers, they would be on their way to a healthy, growing marriage.

When I asked myself what it would be like being married to me, it made me take a long look in the mirror! I saw areas in my life that needed work—plus my respect and admiration for my wife, Jo Beth, soared! This also began the prayer and preparation that led to a sermon series and eventually this book.

As I prepared these marriage commandments, I had two goals in mind: convince and challenge. First, I want to *convince* you that you *can* have a great marriage! Next, I want to *challenge* you to do whatever it takes to achieve that great goal. I sincerely believe that answering the question "What is it like being married to me?" in light of these ten marriage principles will accomplish these goals.

By the way, wherever you are in life—engaged, newly wed, or married for many years; never married, divorced, or widowed—these marriage commandments are for you. They will provide the perfect launch for a new marriage, help you renew a covenant entered into long ago, or help you anticipate and prepare for a future relationship.

Each chapter closes with "Reflecting on Your Relationship," a set of questions to help you apply the principles. If you are married, answer the questions individually, then get together and compare notes. If you are anticipating or preparing for marriage, consider the questions in light of your expectations. Your answers to these questions can provide a standard for measuring compatibility between you and your life partner. If you haven't yet discovered that special person, the answers you give might actually help you understand better the kind of person with whom you would like to spend your life.

Also, you will notice before each chapter "A Personal Word." It's so hard to "let a book go." As it was headed to the publisher, I thought for a moment: *If I could sit down with every reader, and tell each one something before he or she began each chapter, what would it be?* So the personal notes are my last-minute addition to the book. I think they capture "in a nutshell" what I desire you to think about as you read the chapters.

Here's my first "Personal Word." And it concerns the introduction (page 17): *Do not read this book without first reading the introduction! It is a must for understanding the thrust of the book.* It's short, but, oh, so important.

You will find no pious, ministerial meanderings in these dos and don'ts for a lifelong commitment. Instead, I believe you will discover a practical, relevant, humorous, and convicting look at marriage sure to deepen, perhaps even revolutionize, your relationship with your mate. So have fun as you read, and may you be blessed with a marriage touched by God!

ACKNOWLEDGMENTS

Let me express my appreciation to some very special people —my writing team. First, Steve Halliday, gifted author, editor, and friend, performed the challenging task of transforming my spoken words into written ones. His addition of insights, illustrations, and other appropriate materials enhanced the original presentation of these marriage commandments into the book you have before you. I've had the privilege of working with Steve on other projects and can say without a doubt that he "brings a lot to the table." Thank you, Steve!

I also want to thank Wallace Henley, who drew from his vast experience in the ministry and in civic leadership. His understanding of the secular and its effects on the sacred added depth to many of the chapters. Wallace currently serves as one of my associates and has also brought a great wealth of knowledge and wisdom to our ministry.

Thanks also to my administrative assistant, Beverly Gambrell. She served as my liaison during the project and also spent time fine-tuning the manuscript and putting up with my last-minute changes. But I consider her family, so she's used to it!

I would be remiss if I did not take a moment to thank also the many men and women who have written great works on marriage. Through the years I have accumulated a wealth of information from noted authors and speakers. In fact I have included a suggested reading list at the end of the book. It's nowhere near exhaustive, but it includes new works and some classics.

I also want to thank my "preachers." I listen and read from many sources, but some of my regulars are my friends Chuck Swindoll, Jerry Vines, Bill Hybels, and my own son Ed. Every preacher needs a preacher, and I thank these and countless others who inspire and edify me. I have gleaned from their wisdom and counsel, and for that I am most grateful.

Finally, I want to express my personal appreciation to the folks at Moody Publishers. I knew it from afar, but now I know it firsthand: Moody is indeed "the name you can trust."

TEN PRINCIPLES FOR A SUCCESSFUL MARRIAGE

Marriage exposes and reveals who we really are. That's because when we say "I do," we enter a covenant relationship with our marriage partner. In business, partners seal their relationship with a *contract,* enforceable by law. In marriage, two people enter into a *covenant* with one another and with God. This marriage covenant can best be illustrated by an equilateral triangle. God is at the apex, with the husband and wife at their respective corners on the base. As the marriage partners grow closer to God, they actually grow closer to one another. The result of such a covenant relationship is a fulfilling and dynamic marriage.

When I ask a couple to pledge their love and commitment to one another till death do them part, I'm actually asking them to embrace certain commandments or principles that guarantee a successful marriage. But like the Ten Commandments God gave to Moses on Mount Sinai, these Ten Commandments of Marriage cannot be kept without a spiritual transformation.

The apostle Paul teaches that God's Ten Commandments serve as a diagnostic tool. Like instruments in the hand of a skilled physician, these laws examine and probe our lives, revealing the genetic disease of sin. In fact, the Law literally condemns us, breaking the grave news to us that we all have fallen desperately short of God's holy requirement. That hard truth should drive us to our knees and cause us to look to heaven for an answer to our dilemma—a holy cure that comes only from the Great Physician.

What is the cure? "If we confess our sins, He is faithful and righteous to forgive us our sins and to cleanse us from all unrighteousness" (1 John 1:9). When we confess our sins and repent, we do an "about-face" from our sinful lifestyles. Jesus Christ takes our sin and gives us His righteousness in return. That's what I call a divine, spiritual transformation!

In his book *Renovation of the Heart*, Dallas Willard wrote, "The spiritual renovation and spirituality that comes from Jesus is nothing less than an invasion of natural human reality by a supernatural life 'from above.'" That supernatural gift transforms our spirits and begins the work of conforming us to the very image of Christ (Romans 8:29).

God's will for every man and woman is that Christ be formed in him or her (Galatians 4:19). And as we grow in intimacy with the Lord, His Holy Spirit continually reveals areas of our lives out of harmony with Christ and empowers us to deal with them. That often painful process is perhaps better known as *sanctification*.

Transformation must occur in the covenant of marriage. As our sin and shortcomings are diagnosed in light of the marriage commandments, we confess our sins and receive the cure of Christ and then undergo the ongoing treatment of transformation led by the Holy Spirit.

Of course, God did not give these Ten Commandments of Marriage on Mount Sinai. In fact, you will not find them listed in your Bible. But they are there, within the pages of Scripture. These are ten biblical principles that are best revealed in the intimacy of marriage. For example, an unmarried man or woman may not realize how selfish he is, or how poorly she communicates. But when we live with someone who knows us "warts and all" and accepts and loves us anyway, our shortcomings in areas such as selfishness, anger, communication, or forgiveness will be brought into the light.

Just like the Ten Commandments given to Moses, these Ten Commandments of Marriage will act as a diagnostician, probing and revealing the unhealthy aspects of your marital relationship. So read these chapters, these "commandments," and allow the Holy Spirit to do His work.

A PERSONAL WORD
Thou Shalt Not Be a Selfish Pig

For those of you familiar with the biblical definition of love, this chapter may seem "old hat," a simple review. But whether a review or something new, it is the necessary foundation for understanding the love that serves as the foundation of marriage—a love that is the opposite of selfishness.

—E. Y.

Commandment 1

THOU SHALT NOT BE A SELFISH PIG

One hundred forty-two. That's the number of weddings held in our church last year. I didn't perform all 142, of course, but as a pastor with more than forty years of experience, I've "been to the altar" more times than I can count. Many of the ceremonies have left me with lasting memories—some touching, some quite humorous. But in the middle of all the smiles, laughter, and tears of joy that accompany most weddings, something very serious takes place.

When I perform a wedding, I am asking the couple to promise—before God, family, friends, and me—that they will love and cherish one another. I ask them to pledge to honor and sustain each other in sickness and in health, in poverty and in wealth. I instruct them to put the other's needs and desires before their own and anyone else's, except God's.

These solemn promises make up the wedding vows. So far, every bride and groom standing before me has responded with a heartfelt *"I do!"* But sometimes I wonder if they understand fully what they are promising as they exchange their vows. When I ask the couple to make these promises, I am in reality challenging both partners to embrace ten biblical principles that, if applied, will help their marriage not only to survive but thrive! The task will involve commitment, work, plus a lot of give-and-take, but they (and you) truly can have a marriage that sizzles!

That's the kind of marriage God wants us to have. After all, marriage is His idea. He has a divine purpose and plan for the relationship between a husband and wife. And like all of His plans, it is perfect.

GOD'S PERFECT PLAN

God performed the very first marriage ceremony—a beautiful garden wedding on a perfect day with a perfect man marrying a perfect woman. Adam and Eve had it all.

Just imagine! Adam could truly say to Eve, "You're the *only* girl in the world for me!" And he would never hear from Eve those haunting words, "Let me tell you about the guy I *could* have married."

This first couple enjoyed the perfect love relationship, the kind God intended for a husband and wife to share for a lifetime. Adam and Eve lived for some time in sinless perfection, enjoying a pristine garden where God visited them and walked with them in the cool of the evening. Not even a hint of sin or imperfection marred the picture. The Bible tells us that Adam and Eve walked around the garden naked but felt no shame or embarrassment (Genesis 2:25). And their nakedness went beyond the merely physical; they remained totally transparent with one another and with God.

God had promised this first couple great blessings and had given them the run of the garden . . . with just one condition. "This whole garden is yours," God told Adam, "and you can eat the fruit from any tree or plant—that is, all except one. I have placed one tree in the middle of the garden from which you are *not* to eat. If you do eat from this tree, you will gain the knowledge of good and evil—and you're not equipped to handle the weight of that knowledge. If you eat of that tree, you will die"(vv. 16–17, author's paraphrase).

GOD'S PERFECT PLAN DISRUPTED

Adam and Eve both knew the consequences of disobedience. They realized that God had forbidden them to eat from this single tree. But the devil, using language filled with deception and selfishness, enticed Eve.

"Indeed, has God said, 'You shall not eat from any tree in the garden'? . . . You surely will not surely die!" the serpent hissed. "For God knows that [when] you eat from it your eyes will be opened, and you will be like God, knowing good and evil" (3:1, 4–5).

You know the rest of the story. Adam and Eve ate from the forbidden tree, and with their disobedience a divine curse fell on all humanity, resulting in the ultimate tragedy of human history. On that day sin and selfishness permanently stained our existence. At that moment, we lost the perfect fellowship with God that He intended for us to share with Him. At that very instant, every human relationship we would enter, including marriage, shriveled under a divine curse.

HISTORY'S FIRST MARITAL BATTLE

This tragic chain of events set off the first selfishness-induced marital battle in history. When God confronted Adam about his sin, the man responded by blaming his wife: "Lord, it's not my fault. It's hers!" He used different words, but he intended exactly that accusation. The Bible reports that he told God, "The woman whom *You* gave to be with me, she gave me [the fruit], and I ate"(v. 12, italics added). When God turned to Eve to hear her side of the story, she did no better.

She blamed her surroundings and her circumstances. "God, I can't be held responsible for this. The serpent deceived me. Blame *him* for this!"

The whole sordid scene provides a vivid and ugly picture of selfishness in action. It reveals two people giving in to temptation, sinning against God and against one another, then covering for themselves—all in an attempt to avoid accepting the blame and consequences for their sin. The husband blamed the wife and God, while the wife blamed her circumstances.

Sound familiar?

As a consequence, the beautiful marriage relationship that God had designed as a perfect union to benefit both the man and the woman, and to glorify Himself, collapsed into a bitter exchange of accusations and recriminations.

Things have never been the same since.

THE NUMBER ONE PROBLEM IN MARRIAGE

Our first commandment deals with the number one problem in marriage, a setback that cropped up in the garden with Adam and Eve. Since then we've seen it continue all the way to the twenty-first century. It remains the number one problem in your marriage and in mine. What is it?

Selfishness!

We all suffer from the sin of selfishness. It lies at the heart of nearly every marital problem. Marriage counselor Willard F. Harley Jr. wrote,

> Those of us in the business of trying to save marriages struggle daily with cultural beliefs and practices that make our job difficult. The sudden surge of divorces in the 1970s, that has made America the country with the highest divorce rate, has a great deal to do with changes in our basic beliefs. *More to the point, it has to do with a major shift toward self-centeredness.* Beliefs that encourage self-centeredness destroy marriage.[1]

I could not agree more with Dr. Harley. And that's why our first commandment of marriage states: *Thou shalt not be a selfish pig.*

That's about as simple and blunt as you can get. Still, I'm convinced that if every couple walking the aisle took seriously this single principle, a welcome oasis of marital bliss would spread across this nation. Divorce lawyers would have to "take a number" at the unemployment office. I'm beginning to think I should incorporate these exact words into the marriage ceremony: "Thou shalt not be a selfish pig."

This first commandment calls us to do in marriage what the apostle Paul instructs all of us to do: "Do nothing out of selfish ambition or vain conceit, but in humility consider others better than yourselves" (Philippians 2:3 NIV). Sounds easy, doesn't it? But our number one problem, selfishness, makes it tough.

Perhaps we can take some positive steps toward incorporating this commandment into our marriages if we look at the problem of selfishness as a disease.

THE DISEASE CALLED *PIGITIS*

I like to refer to the disease of selfishness as *pigitis*. If you've ever seen a pigpen, you get the idea. I saw my first pigpen as a boy. I had imagined a corral filled with shiny little "Porky Pigs," but I saw quite the opposite. The pen overflowed with dozens of chunky beasts, all nuzzling slop with muddy snouts. Those pigs lost themselves in the mire, even shoving aside any other pig that tried to nudge in—including their own piglets!

You don't have to be the world's leading physician to diagnose *pigitis*. Wherever you see someone with his snout so mired in his own interests that he forgets everyone else, you see an infected person.

I wonder: Do you have *pigitis?*

SYMPTOMS OF *PIGITIS*

If you're not sure, look for the symptoms. Most illnesses reveal visible, physical symptoms. Selfish *pigitis* is no different. Its symptoms are as obvious as those of chicken pox!

Do a little "self-diagnosis" as you consider each of the symptoms listed below. Ask yourself, "To what degree has this symptom of selfish *pigitis* infected me?" To help you remember these symptoms, I'm going to use the "itis" of *pigitis* as an acrostic. The four symptoms are: immaturity, time choices, insensitivity, and stubbornness.

Immaturity

Jo Beth and I dated for more than six years before we married. In hindsight, I believe that whatever we felt for one another on the day we married had more in common with "puppy love" than with genuine, mature love. We had to start growing up.

Forty-three years later, the process continues!

What do I mean by "puppy love"? Puppy love is an immature form of the love dynamic that binds two people together. When we are in "puppy love," we want to be with a person because of how he or she makes us feel. In puppy love, our emotional and physical needs take a central place in the relationship. And like those pigs in the slop, we push aside anyone who doesn't satisfy and gratify our needs.

Many of us start with puppy love. Nothing wrong with that; it can be fun and enjoyable. But unless puppy love grows into mature love, the marriage will struggle and may not survive the trying times. And if you build your marital relationship on puppy love, you'll end up living a dog's life!

Consider the contrasts between puppy love and mature love in the chart on the next page.

PUPPY LOVE VERSUS MATURE LOVE

PUPPY LOVE	MATURE LOVE
Focuses on receiving	Seeks to give to the other person
Impatient, self-centered	Patient in spite of the other's flaws
Tends to outbursts of anger	Responds gently and appropriately to irritants
Self-protective, because it insists on meeting its needs above all	Transparent and vulnerable

The answer to the problem of puppy love is maturity—and that means living, as Paul puts it in Ephesians 5:15, with "wisdom" toward one another. We are to live and conduct our marriages as mature men and women in Christ. Unfortunately, however, far too many of us never grow beyond immaturity in either our married or our spiritual lives. While Jesus tells us to be child*like,* immature people remain child*ish.*

Sociologists and psychologists agree that America suffers a crisis of fatherhood partly because so many men never grow beyond adolescence. Their bodies age, but their minds still think like immature kids.

Men (and women too) experiment constantly with new ways to satisfy their desires. But even the most immature can acquire wisdom as they study and embrace God's principles.

Jo Beth and I had a lot of growing up to do when we married. Though we are now grandparents, we are still growing as individuals and in our relationship. And I can honestly say that growing and maturing together has yielded a life even more exciting and rewarding than those early days of puppy love!

Time Choices

The apostle Paul tells us to "redeem" our time (Ephesians 5:16 KJV). Literally, we are to "buy up" all the opportunities time can bring us.

I enjoy playing golf. So whenever I get the opportunity, I visit a nearby course to play or at least hit some practice balls. I've become casually acquainted with a man who seems to be hitting golf balls at the practice range every time I show up. Unless by some great coincidence he just happens to arrive at the course when I'm there, he apparently spends a great deal of time golfing. It seems as though he is already there whenever I arrive and is still there when I leave. He must hit hundreds of balls every day.

I can't help but wonder: *How does this man spend his time?* Does he have a neglected wife and kids at home, waiting for their husband and father to return from the golf course?

One man recently told me, "I struggle with selfishness in my marriage in the area of leisure time. I grew up loving sports, and would spend hours watching it on television. During the first several years of my marriage, I noticed that many of my evenings were spent not with my wife but with ESPN."

Because this young man did not want to be a selfish pig, he made a tough choice. He decided to get rid of cable—and he called it one of the best decisions he ever made for his marriage! How much time could we men gain to spend quality time with our wives if only we would turn off the television? I have to confess, I can channel surf with the best of them, especially when it comes to sports and news networks. But I'm convinced, men, that if we'll just turn off the TV, we will have the opportunity to gain more joy in increased intimacy with our wives.

It's easy to spend our time on our careers, our hobbies, our avocations, and other self-gratifying activities—all at the expense of our marriages. I can't begin to tell you the number of people I've known whose marriages have suffered because one or both partners became "too busy" to make time for their relationship. The husband and wife seemed to inhabit different worlds. They lived together, yet never took the time for one another. The best that either could hope for from the other was "leftovers." Leftover food might make a tasty meal, but leftover time creates a bland relationship.

Insensitivity

"If I had known he was so insensitive and unfeeling, I never would have married him!" I've heard this complaint from unhappy wives more times than I care to count. I sympathize with the feelings that spark such harsh words. They often come from a frustrated wife who feels unappreciated, who believes that her husband doesn't care about her needs or what she's thinking or feeling.

Insensitivity kills a marriage and can destroy any kind of relationship. It's hard to live with, work with, or associate with an insensitive person. No one wants to spend time with someone who doesn't listen or give any consideration to the feelings or thoughts of others.

In Ephesians 5:17, Paul provides a model of what *sensitivity* looks like: "So then do not be foolish, but understand what the will of the Lord is." Two contrasting words take the spotlight in this verse: *foolish* and *understand*. This verse tells us that foolishness follows a lack of understanding.

Understanding depends upon sensitivity. We need it in our relationship with the Lord and with other people, especially our spouse. Sensitivity means seeking to understand the other person's thoughts, feelings, and needs.

Let's take a look at this kind of sensitivity in action. Mark and Laurie have been married for almost ten years. Mark owns a small business, selling sporting goods. The business provides him great personal fulfillment and a healthy family income.

Long before she met Mark, Laurie discovered her love for oil painting. Through the years, she developed her passion into a profitable sideline business.

But then three kids came along in four years. As the diapers and high chairs multiplied, Laurie's time for painting faded. The couple had always planned for Mark to be the "breadwinner," allowing Laurie her desire to be a homemaker. But this busy mom gradually discovered that her love for painting provided a welcome creative outlet that helped to balance her day. Her overwhelming household duties, however, soon gave her fewer and fewer opportunities to paint.

Mark sensed Laurie's need to express her artistic gift and after giving the situation much thought, he decided to cut back on his number of clients in order to help his wife pursue her artistic career. Laurie now has access to a small gallery that provides her with refreshing breaks from her routine.

And Mark? He takes care of the children and household chores every Tuesday, Thursday morning, and Saturday afternoon. Through his sensitivity to his wife's needs and his choice to act selflessly, Mark discovered a cherished part of his life. Had he decided to act like a selfish pig, he would have denied both his wife and himself an enormous amount of happiness.

Ask yourself a couple of questions. As a wife, are you sensitive to your husband when he's in the middle of a pressure-packed time at the office? As a husband, are you sensitive to your wife when she's struggling with her boss or with the children? Are you sensitive to one another during those times when you just don't feel like "yourselves"?

Insensitivity is a classic symptom of *pigitis*. It causes us to live foolishly—and our marriages suffer.

Stubbornness

It seems only fitting that one symptom of *pigitis* is stubbornness, also known as "pigheadedness." And nowhere do we see stubbornness in marriage more clearly than in the area of submission. Paul uncovers this problem in Ephesians 5:22, when he writes that wives are to submit to their husbands as they would to the Lord.

Some husbands believe this verse puts them "in charge," and no matter what conflict or disagreement arises, what *they* say goes. Only one problem: That's *not* what this verse means!

Right before the apostle says that wives should submit to their husbands, he states that *all* Christians should submit to one another, motivated by reverence for Christ. We are all to lay aside the stubbornness that characterizes our fallen natures and consider the needs of others. Sometimes, this includes husbands submitting to their wives.

A few years ago, Bob and Betty began a practice that revolutionized their marriage. They began to ask each other: "What says, 'I love you' to you?" They committed to act on the answers they heard and thus found the key to *mutual submission.*

They stumbled onto this practice early in their marriage. Betty had long assumed that, more than anything else, Bob wanted a clean house when he came home from work. So every afternoon before he arrived home, she would rush through the house like a whirlwind, cleaning everything in sight. She would always greet Bob and follow him into the house, waiting for his praise for her immaculate housework— but it never came. Understandably, she began to resent Bob's lack of appreciation and diagnosed him as suffering from an acute case of *pigitis.*

One day she'd had enough. With fire in her eyes, she confronted Bob. As they talked, Betty discovered that Bob really didn't care if the house was clean when he got home. He just wanted to know what was for dinner! The meal didn't even have to be ready; they could be ordering pizza, for all he cared. What said "I love you" to Bob was not a clean house but a happy wife with dinner plans.

What a revelation (and relief) to Betty! From that day on, Bob and Betty began asking the question "What says 'I love you' to you?"

No better or more harmonious marriages exist than those in which both partners submit to one another as they would to the Lord. This doesn't mean disagreements and conflicts never erupt. It does mean, however, that ultimate peace reigns in the marriage because both the husband and the wife consciously choose to put the other first in all decision-making.

DIAGNOSIS AND TREATMENT OF *PIGITIS*

It's time to look in the mirror. Do you suffer from *pigitis?* Do you see yourself in one or more of the symptoms just described: immaturity, insensitivity, or stubbornness? Do you tend to misuse your time or give it to your personal activities or interests, leaving your mate the leftovers? If you answered "yes" to any of these questions, then you suffer from *pigitis.*

The truth is, most of us do.

Selfish *pigitis* has made many marriages so sick that the relationship needs an intensive care unit. Their union has all the characteristics of anemia. They've lost the passion, fun, and effectiveness for God they once had together. They feel bored and unfilled in the marriage and even "numb" toward one another.

In one sense, that's not all bad news. If you recognize such problems in your marriage, you've already taken a giant step toward making positive changes. It will take hard work and perseverance, but you *can* overcome selfish *pigitis.*

To help you do that, I would recommend that you get some PEP (another fun acrostic). The treatment for *pigitis* includes three ingredients: *p*riorities, *e*xpectations, and *p*atterns.

Priorities

Get on the same page. That's the first ingredient in treating selfish *pigitis.* Many marriages go for decades without so much as a word spoken about individual and mutual priorities. When two people don't work toward goals important to both, selfishness easily comes into play. And usually the goals of one become dominant.

The key to getting on the same page? Set your priorities *together.* Take the time to write down your personal list of priorities in such areas as friendships, work, church, money, vacation, and children. Once you've each made your list, compare them. See where they overlap and where they differ. Then sit down and work out the differences. Remember, if the goal is to get on the same page, that requires mutual "give-and-take."

Would you like a fun and effective way to do this? Then consider going on a personal retreat, just you and your mate. You don't have to go far away or spend a lot of money. Just take a couple of days and go somewhere special to the two of you where you can work through your priorities. And spend some time enjoying one another!

Expectations

Our dog, Sonny, had a tick problem. Have you ever observed one of those little suckers? And that's exactly what they are—ticks survive by sucking the blood out of their "host" animal. Well, let me tell you, Sonny was a *great* host! He wore special collars and got dipped to kill the little parasites, but somehow ticks would still attach themselves to Sonny and have a feast. Their "feeding frenzies" caused them to swell up to several times their normal size. Many a tick lived a full life by feeding off of our Sonny.

What do Sonny's ticks have to do with marriage? Every couple that comes to the altar bring their own set of expectations. Whenever I stand before a bride and groom, I have the uncanny ability to read their minds. As I watch them look into each other's eyes, I know what *both* of them are thinking: *This person is going to meet all my needs.*

That's when the trouble begins.

I call this a "tick on the dog" relationship. Problem is, in far too many marriages, you have *two ticks and no dog!* Neither partner's legitimate needs get met, as each tries to feed off the other.

Certainly it's normal to have some expectations of your mate and marriage. That's part of the "I do" promise. It's vital, however, that every couple clearly communicate their expectations. That's why the second ingredient of our treatment for *pigitis* is *defining expectations.*

Most of us go about this all wrong. We survey the marriages we know anything about and reach a general conclusion: *This is what a good marriage must be like.* I might look at the relationship between my mother and father or observe other couples I've known, read about, or seen on television and from this information try to determine what a marriage ought to look like. This deeply flawed method of understanding expectations in marriage can lead to disappointment, even disaster.

We build healthy marriages when we sit down with our spouse and define our needs and goals as a team. We say, "This is what we want our marriage to be like." In other words, we get our expectations together. "This is what we expect out of marriage. These are our goals for our relationship."

Try doing this on the personal "marriage retreat" I suggested earlier. Get away with your mate and think and talk through your expectations and goals. If you'll do this, you'll less likely focus on yourself and more likely focus on meeting the needs of your spouse. And you'll be well on your way to getting over selfish *pigitis.*

Patterns

The final ingredient to *pigitis* treatment involves *getting your lifestyle patterns together.* When two people marry, they bring into the relationship different ways of dealing with life. Every home is unique, and we bring those unique lifestyle patterns with us to the altar. Some of these patterns may need to be broken, while others embraced.

Suppose a husband comes from a family that showed its affection much more than did his wife's. Or perhaps the members of his family are very frugal while his wife's spend readily.

Take time with your mate to get your lifestyle patterns together. How will you make decisions? How will you resolve conflict? How will you handle money? How will you discipline your children?

Jo Beth and I grew up together. When we married, we already knew each other pretty well. Still, we came from different families and lifestyle patterns. We had to establish our own lifestyle patterns when we married. You must do the same if you're going to rid your marriage of *pigitis*.

THE ROAD TO RECOVERY

How do we know when we're on the road to recovery from *pigitis?* How do we know when we're cured?

Love. Love is the answer.

Let's clarify that word—one that suffers from overuse in our society. We "love" everything from people, to pets, to pastimes, to pizza. The word has become shallow and has lost much of its rich depth of meaning. It's been "watered down." So if "love" brings health back into our marriages—and assures us that our *pigitis* is under control—let's take a moment to restore value to the meaning of love. There's no better place to find the true meaning of love than in the Bible. God is love, and in His Word He has given us clear instructions about life, including love and marriage.

The New Testament contains an array of Greek terms that we translate with the single word *love*. Each of these Greek words describes a unique kind of love, or a different depth or aspect of love. Since America's word *love* lacks depth of meaning, let's spend some time looking at these biblical "loves." Let's consider what we could call *feelings* love, *friendship* love, and *forever* love.

When your marriage contains all three of these loves, you'll know that you're cured of *pigitis* and on your way to a sizzling marriage.

Feelings Love

I clearly remember how I felt when I first fell in love with Jo Beth—my heart beating as if I'd just run a four-minute mile and my stomach churning like a whole colony of butterflies had moved in. She was like a magnet to me. I felt drawn to her all the time! I felt as lovesick as the man described by the anonymous poet:

> I climbed up the door
> And shut the stairs;
> I said my shoes and took off my prayers.
> I shut off the bed and climbed into the light.
> And all because—
> *She kissed me good night!*

I can identify with the poor guy in this poem. He had a bad case of what I call "feelings love," or romantic love. The Greek term for this type of love is *eros,* the kind of erotic love that gets top billing in romance novels and movies.

By the way, erotic love is not "bad"; after all, it was God's idea. Read the Song of Solomon and you'll see how God meant erotic or feelings love to function within marriage.

This type of love involves "chemistry" between a husband and wife—an exciting mixture of passion, physical attraction, acts of affection, and sexuality. Romantic love is a wonderful gift from God to be shared between a man and woman committed to one another in marriage. It's not only an enjoyable part of marriage, it's a *vital* part.

Ask any marriage counselor to name the question most asked by husbands and wives, and he'll probably say something like, "How can I restore the passion and excitement to my life and to my marriage?" When people say the romance or the "spark" has gone from their marriages, the problem is the fading of feelings love.

Certainly it's not easy to maintain passion and excitement in marriage. But torches can be relit. You can restore romantic love to your marriage. You can indeed have a marriage that sizzles. How? Let me give you some practical steps to help you restore the "feelings" to your relationship.

- Give attention to your relationship. I always advise couples to keep dating each other. Husbands need to "court" their wives with the same dedication they needed to win their love. Wives should make their husbands feel as special as a knight in shining armor.

- Activate your will. Even if you don't feel the same emotions you once did, activate your will to do the things you naturally did back in those days of passionate, romantic love. Imagine your life as a train. Your will is the locomotive and your emotions are the caboose. Once the locomotive starts moving on the tracks, the caboose follows. So, don't concentrate on feelings. Feelings are important, but healthy emotions can't be generated by feelings alone. Commit to *actions that benefit your mate*, and then watch as the feelings rekindle.

- Stay on the tracks. Consider the following tracks laid out in Scripture. The first obligation we have as husband and wife is obvious: *Love your mate as a cherished husband or wife* (Ephesians 5:25; Titus 2:4). The Bible instructs both husbands and wives to love one another. Unfortunately, some people have trouble with that mandate. So the second level of our track may be a bit easier for them: *Love your mate as a fellow believer* (1 Peter 3:8). If you still don't think you can fill this bill, then do your best to comply with the third biblical level: *Love your mate as a neighbor* (Matthew 22:39). If this still feels like too tall of an order, Jesus has one last directive for you: *Love your mate as an enemy* (Matthew 5:44). The Lord teaches us to love our enemies. If you can't love your mate at least as much as you love your enemies, then you probably have some problems that go beyond the marital realm. Your first order of business is to make sure of your relationship with the Lord, because without that, no amount of relationship seminars or how-to books will help your marital troubles.

Let's move on to the next kind of love necessary to ward off selfish *pigitis.* There is much more to marriage than romantic love. While I grant that this is a vital, fun, and enjoyable stage, your marriage will suffer if you have only one-third of the love it needs. More than one marriage has failed because a couple neglected to move beyond feelings love.

Friendship Love

"Irving Jones and Jesse Brown were married on October 24. So ends a friendship that began in school days." So announced the church bulletin after the Joneses' wedding.[2] I hope that Irving and Jesse continued their friendship, despite the gloomy declaration!

The Greek word for "friendship love" is *philia.* Hence *Phila*delphia is called "the city of brotherly love." *Philia* refers to affection and bonding between two individuals. *Eros,* or feelings love, results in a person falling "madly" or "blindly" in love, as if something irresistible in the other person pulls the smitten lover into the relationship. But *philia*, friendship love, carries the idea of choice—an act of the will.

The best marriages in the world are those in which the partners not only "fall in love" but choose one another as best friend. Think for a moment about the best friend you ever had. Remember how you could tell this person anything without fear of judgment or rejection? You felt safe to share your secret thoughts, deepest feelings, and innermost desires.

In such a marriage, the husband and wife can honestly say they married their "best friend." Such couples have so much in common that they enjoy one another's company, even apart from marriage's sexual aspect.

Physical attraction frequently gets the attention of a man and woman for one another, but couples who count each other best friends consciously choose such a relationship. One influential author says it this way:

> Noel and I, in obedience to Jesus Christ, have pursued as passionately as we could the deepest, most lasting joys possible. All too imperfectly, all too half-heartedly at times, we have staked our own joy in the joy of each other. And we can testify together: for those who marry, this is the path to the heart's desire. . . . As each pursues joy in the joy of the other and fulfills a God-ordained role, the mystery of marriage as a parable of Christ and the church becomes manifest for His great glory and for our great joy.[3]

I've often said that marriage is friendship that catches fire. If your marriage includes "feelings" love and "friendship" love, rejoice; it's on the mend from *pigitis*.

Forever Love

Feelings and friendship love are both based, at least to some degree, on mutual enjoyment, satisfaction, and fulfillment. I've found much happiness in the romantic and friendship love Jo Beth and I share, and I trust she has found the same thing. But "forever love" cares so much for another that he or she gives with no expectation of return.

In its purest form, "forever" love has been demonstrated by God. He has poured out this unconditional love in sending His Son, Jesus Christ. We cannot deserve it and we can give nothing in return that equals it.

The Greek word for such love is *agape*. The term is so rare that it doesn't appear much in Greek literature outside the Bible. It's as if the word had been created and reserved solely to express God's love for us.

In marriage, this type of love endures the ups and downs of feelings love and the highs and lows of friendship love. This is the love that transcends romantic feelings and surges of devotion. It is not based on feelings but on an enduring commitment. *Eros* love is a matter of the body; *philia* has to do with the soul; but *agape* is an issue of the spirit.

Many couples try to make it with a one-third, or, at best, a two-thirds marriage. Many have a physical relationship only and when the fire dies, the marriage ends. Others have the physical and the friendship, but the day comes when the friendship sours and the marriage terminates.

But husbands and wives who enjoy a "three-thirds" marriage have a whole relationship. No matter what happens at the other levels, *agape* love sustains the marriage and gives it depth and vitality.

The Bible provides a classic description of *agape* love through the following words and phrases (adapted from 1 Corinthians 13:4–7):

Patient

Kind

Not jealous

Not boastful and arrogant

Does not behave inappropriately

Does not seek its own interests primarily

Does not hold grudges

Does not rejoice in wrong but in truth

Carries all burdens

Not cynical and distrusting

Hopes in all situations

Endures everything that comes against it

From time to time, I see how I'm doing in each of these characteristics of *agape* love. I ask myself if I'm patient, kind, jealous, boastful, or arrogant to Jo Beth—you get the picture. I encourage you to give yourself the same test regarding your spouse or loved one. If you're honest, you will discover areas in which you, like I, need to improve.

"Feelings" love makes marriage exciting. "Friendship" love brings fun and interest to the relationship. But these loves wax and wane, surge and retreat. *Agape* love, however, remains constant and makes the marriage secure. It takes "forever" love to crowd out our self-centeredness and to restore the passion and friendship that cures selfish *pigitis*. And only God can give us this kind of love.

WELL WORTH THE EFFORT

In a recent interview, Oprah Winfrey spoke with Billy Graham about his marriage of fifty-six years to his wife, Ruth.

"What's the secret to your wonderful marriage?" asked Oprah.

Dr. Graham simply answered, "We are happily incompatible."

What was he saying? The great evangelist meant that while he and his wife are different, they have happily reconciled their differences. Billy and Ruth Graham have learned how to overcome their own selfishness and consider each other as more important. That's our first marriage commandment in action. They illustrate how this commandment provides the foundation for a happy, successful marriage.

While marriage isn't always easy, it's always worth the effort. In fact, outside of a relationship with Jesus Christ, marriage is the most sacred and most fabulous relationship God offers. When a man and woman learn how to put aside their own selfishness and give one another top priority, then their marriage can fill up with passion, satisfaction, and power.

REFLECTING ON YOUR RELATIONSHIP

1. In what specific areas of your relationship with your spouse (or loved one) do you find yourself behaving or thinking selfishly?

2. What specific symptoms of *pigitis* can you identify in yourself?

3. What kinds of expectations do you have for your marriage and spouse? How can you begin communicating those expectations to him or her?

4. Take the "love test of 1 Corinthians 13." Ask yourself if you're patient, kind, boastful, etc., to your spouse. In what area(s) do you need to improve?

A PERSONAL WORD
Thou Shalt Cut the Apron Strings

When we stand at the altar we, in effect, are telling our mate that he or she is number one. But if we're still attached to parents or past places and people, our spouse in reality may not even be in our top ten. To leave, cleave, and become one, you have to cut the strings.

—E. Y.

Commandment 2

THOU SHALT CUT
THE APRON STRINGS

During a group session, a counselor asked three men, "What would you do if you knew you had only four weeks to live?"

"That's easy!" the first man answered. "I'd go to Las Vegas and have a good time spending all my money. You can't take it with you, so I might as well live it up before I go."

The second guy, the group's humanitarian, said, "I'd go out and serve my fellowman any way I could. I would minister to people and try to make their lives better."

The counselor turned to the third man and waited for his response. Without hesitation, the man answered, "I would move in with my mother-in-law and I would stay with her every minute of every day for the whole four weeks."

"That's a little odd," the counselor replied. "Why would you do that when there are more enjoyable and productive ways to spend the last weeks of your life?"

"Because," the man answered, "those would be the four longest weeks of my life!"

My apologies to any mother-in-law who might be reading this, but you know more than anyone else how mother-in-law jokes abound in our culture. We laugh at them, not necessarily out of disrespect but because so often they contain small elements of truth.

Some marriages enjoy mutual love and respect between in-laws. The parents know when to leave their children alone and let them work out their own marital issues. Sadly, however, many other marriages have to endure the constant meddling of parents-in-law or other relatives.

Interference in marriage, of course, doesn't come only from well-meaning in-laws. It also can come from friends, other family members, even ex-spouses, ex-boyfriends, and ex-girlfriends. Yet the last thing a married couple needs is external or internal interference—which brings us to our second commandment for marriage: *Thou shalt cut the apron strings.*

MARRIAGE: GOD'S PERFECT DESIGN

When the Frenchman Auguste Bartholdi designed the Statue of Liberty, he knew he had to structure it properly. The winds in New York Harbor would push and tug at the huge mass of copper and rip it apart if the statue weren't built right. The monument could even collapse under its own weight if its components weren't correctly placed in relationship.

Bartholdi therefore turned to Gustave Eiffel, a structural engineer who built the famous tower bearing his name. For the Statue of Liberty, Eiffel constructed a core of steel and iron and then attached frame supports to its central portion. Eiffel's knowledge of which parts should adjoin and which should have separate loads made possible the beloved statue that welcomes the world to America.

In a similar way, God carefully designed the structure of

marriage to hold up in every type of storm. His key design principle for strong marriages can be summed up in two words: *leaving* and *cleaving*.

Even in marriage, certain elements must be joined for the sake of strength, while certain other components must be separated, lest their combined weight bring down the whole structure.

GOD'S BLUEPRINT FOR MARRIAGE

Right at the beginning of Adam and Eve's relationship as husband and wife, God told the pair, "Therefore shall a man leave his father and his mother, and shall cleave unto his wife: and they shall be one flesh" (Genesis 2:24 KJV).

Five times this command appears in the Bible.[1] Now, whenever God says *anything,* we know it's important. When He states something twice, we may put a star by it or underline it. But *five* times! Do you get the idea He's trying to get our full attention? When God considers something significant enough to say it five times, we can be certain it's vitally important. We'd better get it right!

God's statement to Adam and Eve contains three crucial words: *leave, cleave,* and *flesh.* Understanding these three words provides the key to understanding the way God meant for marriage to function. I believe that all marital problems stem from the husband's or wife's failure to fully follow the instructions in Genesis 2:24 to leave, cleave, and become one flesh. So if we can get this right, we're on our way to healthier, stronger, and happier marriages.

A MAN AND A WOMAN COME TOGETHER

In our culture, when an eligible man and woman meet and express a mutual interest, a dating relationship often begins. During this courtship period the couple discovers differences and similarities in goals, desires, dreams, and even likes and dislikes. Eventually, they may unite in marriage.

Coming Together . . . Like Glue

When this happens, God instructs the husband and wife to leave the parental influence of childhood and youth in order to cleave to one another. "Cleave" is our word for "glue." And not just glue—super glue!

I've learned the hard way to be very careful when working with super glue. To her credit, Jo Beth did try to warn me. When I told her I "accidentally" stuck my thumb to my index finger, she lovingly and patiently (and a little too slowly, I might add) walked into the bathroom and got some strong-smelling liquid that helped separate my fingers. I came away with a whole new understanding of "one flesh." With enough super glue, the bond would have been too tight to break without damaging the flesh of one or both fingers.

That's how strong the bond of marriage is meant to be.

Coming Together . . . Like Candles

Most of us have attended a wedding in which the bride and groom light a "unity" candle. On the altar sits a candle stand with three candles—one large one between two smaller ones. At the appropriate time in the service, the bride and groom take the smaller candles, representing their individual lives, and together light the larger candle. When they finish lighting this "unity" candle, they blow out theirs, symbolizing that they are no longer two individuals but one.

I must confess that I don't believe this imagery best expresses what actually happens when two people marry. I believe that God intends the marriage partner to keep his or her own identity. The bride is still the bride, and the groom, the groom; they are still distinctly male and female; each keeps his and her own personality, needs, and gifts. But in marriage all their separateness bonds together to create something stronger and deeper than what existed before. They are now husband and wife!

When a man and woman "leave and cleave," they become one. This is what I like to call "God's divine math." One plus one equals one! There is now one flesh, one agenda, one marriage unit.

If every couple had a clear understanding of what they are to leave and to what they are to cleave, every marriage could enjoy the structural dependability that God designed in the beginning. No storm could bring it down!

LEAVING PARENTS

What does God mean when He tells us we are to leave "father and mother"? Let me first say what He is *not* saying.

By no means is God suggesting that we terminate our relationships with our parents when we marry. He simply wants us to know that our parents are no longer the preeminent figures in our lives; our mates now hold that exalted position.

Certainly every mother occupies a place that no other woman can take in the life of her son. But once he marries, she is no longer the number one woman in his life. That spot is now reserved for his wife. Likewise, while no one can ever take the place of a daughter's "daddy," the woman's husband, not her father, is the most important man in her world.

Married couples must remember they have entered a relationship in which they commit to honor one another, tend to one another's needs, obey one another, and keep themselves for one another in every way. Children who get married need to "leave" and the parents need to let them go.

I call this process "cutting the apron strings." There are two primary apron strings every couple must cut.

1. Cutting the "Counseling String"

Because we so often depend on our parents for advice, the first apron string I suggest severing is the *counseling string*. You can tell your parents to cut that string—or give them this section of the book and let them read these two points. After all, it's best that parents initiate this cut. So these two points are written primarily to parents.

As they grow up, our children need our advice. And it feels good being needed. But after they marry, we need to back off and let our married children work out their problems on their own.

As a parent myself, I know this is tough to do. My oldest son, Ed, was the first of our boys to marry. If I foresaw a problem coming or thought I knew what he ought to do in a certain situation, I always wanted to butt in and set him straight on how to be the ideal husband! But Jo Beth would punch me in the ribs or give me "that look," reminding me that I knew very little about being the ideal husband.

Likewise, when conflicts or issues arise between married couples, they should never first call mom and dad for advice. Rather, they should go to one another and, using the principles laid out in God's Word, prayerfully try to work out their own problems, seeking outside counsel only if necessary.

So does this mean that an in-law should never offer counsel or advice? Of course not. At times, every family needs outside counsel. If you are a parent or parent-in-law, you can offer valuable perspective. Remember, however, wise parents understand they must listen to *all* sides, including the position of their in-law children. As you listen quietly, pray, and encourage, the day comes when you will discover you are genuinely loved, respected, and heard.

Now, to the person who has left (or is leaving) mother and father: Setting up a household does not mean you must terminate the relationship with your parents. You are to leave them, not forsake them nor forgo all their influence. After we marry, we are still to obey the Lord's command to honor our mother and father. The hard-won experience of parents can still play a vital role in the lives of their married children. The Bible contains many wonderful examples of just that.

Consider Naomi, the consummate mother-in-law who had a beautiful relationship with her daughter-in-law Ruth. And recall Jethro, the father-in-law of Moses. Jethro pulled Moses aside and told him he was working himself to death. He advised him how to be a more efficient leader and administrator. Moses followed his father-in-law's advice and made his life and his service to God much more effective.

It's not always easy for parents to cut the ties and allow their children to leave and start their own marriages and families. Likewise, it's hard for some married children to leave behind the security of the homes and lifestyles in which they grew up. But if you want a healthy marriage, you must leave the "safety net" of your parents behind and create your own "home, sweet home."

2. Cutting the Economic Strings

Because some married couples stay too closely attached to parents and in-laws for reasons related to money, I suggest that parents cut *economic strings*. To not do so may make the couple dependent or even resentful.

When Elizabeth's husband died, leaving her a fortune, she lavished her married children and their families with homes, cars, and every luxury they desired. But Elizabeth's acts of generosity always came with a catch. Every time one of her children made a decision she questioned, Elizabeth would say, "After all I've done for you, you still won't do what I want." Her children became heavily dependent on her and so were easy to manipulate—and not surprisingly, they became extremely resentful.

Ann and Bill had a healthier view. They discussed the level of support their children would receive from them when the kids reached adulthood. They determined they would help their children get established, then pull back so the kids could support themselves. Ann and Bill paid most college expenses and helped both their son and daughter buy their first homes. Then, although they had plenty of money, Ann and Bill reduced their financial support for the children and their families. With the economic string cut, Ann and Bill's family enjoyed a relationship free of manipulation and guilt.

Without knowing it, Ann and Bill followed the weaning method of the eagle. The mother bird nudges a baby out of the nest before the eaglet learns to fly. As the immature bird zooms toward the ground, the mother swoops under it and carries it on her back. Gradually, through this terrifying exercise, the baby eagle learns to flap its wings and support itself in the air. In a similar way, financial "weaning" can occur within a human parent-child relationship.

God calls married children to "leave" Mom and Dad. Much of this can be accomplished through cutting counseling and economic strings. But successfully married couples learn that they need to leave more than just their parents.

LEAVING "PAST PEOPLE"

Several years ago Willie Nelson and Julio Iglesias sang a popular tune, "To All the Girls I've Loved Before." I can still hear them praising all their past girlfriends as they crooned.

Willie and Julio notwithstanding, men have to leave the girls they loved before, and women must leave their previous boyfriends. It's a huge mistake to actively hang on to the memories of past loves. Husbands and wives must put those relationships behind them and give their total affections and feelings of love to their mates.

Hanging on to all the girls or guys you've loved before can

lead to the "greener grass" syndrome. It's only a matter of time before conflict erupts in your marriage. If you don't "leave" your past loves, you'll feel tempted to mentally compare your partner with that person from your past. Thoughts such as, *If only I had married Sally instead,* or *I know Bill would have acted differently in this situation,* can drive a wedge between a husband and wife.

You and I both know there really is no "greener grass." Every meadow has its share of beggar lice, blighted spots, and thorns. So how do you get greener grass? By watering the grass you already have! Irrigate and cultivate what you have with your mate, rather than gazing longingly at former relationships.

LEAVING "PAST PROBLEMS"

No one can successfully cleave in marriage without first leaving problems of the past. Some individuals discover only after they get married that they can't function because of previous failures or abuse suffered in an earlier relationship.

When the baggage filled with those past problems sits in the middle of the room—whether in the honeymoon suite or the bedroom at home—it blocks everything. The problems of the past adversely affect conversation between a husband and wife, their sexual relationship, and their trust.

Two years shy of thirty, Rose still carried the guilt of her high school years when her promiscuity had led to three abortions. When she married John she thought she had dealt with her past. But on their wedding night as her husband caressed her, all she could think about was her lurid history. She stiffened and became cold.

If we want our marriages to reflect well on God, it is essential that we leave our past mistakes right where they belong: in the past! We need to leave the things we've done and those things done to us at the foot of the cross. We have to move on.

You don't know how bad it is for me, you may be thinking.

I made such a horrible mistake that I can't forgive myself. I just can't forget this and leave it in the past!

Would you like the key to getting rid of those footlockers full of past junk? If so, you'll find it in the principle of confession and repentance. When we confess our sin to God and turn away from it, He is more than able and willing to forgive us and cleanse us from *all* the trash from our past (see 1 John 1:9).

Do you know what that word "all" means? It means *all!* Everything! God doesn't pick and choose which sins He'll forgive and which ones He'll hold against us. He literally cleanses us inside and out, declaring each sin we've committed forgiven and divinely forgotten. Do you know what God then does with our sin? The Bible says He casts our sin into the depths of the sea (Micah 7:19).

So lay your sins and mistakes—the ones you committed in high school, the ones you committed in college, and the ones you've committed since then—at the foot of the Cross. Then *leave* them there for God to pick up and bury at the bottom of the sea.

LEAVING "PAST PLACES"

I'm pretty sure that my wife and I are somewhat rare. We have known each other nearly all our lives. In fact, we first met in the church nursery. No, we weren't dropping off our children; we *were* the children!

I like to tell folks that Jo Beth was working in the nursery and I was in a crib, but that's not true. We grew up in the same small town, attended the same church, and graduated from the same schools. So whenever I talk about a special event or friends from high school, she knows exactly what I'm talking about—she was there, and vice versa.

If you share that type of history with your mate, it's OK to talk about past places. But I would guess that most people met their husband or wife a little later in life than during the diaper years! Most of you "had a life" before you met your mate. So when you talk about special places or events from your premarriage days, especially if your mate was not present, you run the high risk of making him or her feel left out or estranged.

Alienation from a husband or wife can result whenever we fail to leave the things that prevent us from cleaving to our mate. What kind of things? Take your pick:

- an unhealthy emotional or material dependency on parents
- the people who once dominated your relationships
- the problems brought on by past behaviors
- the places where you had experiences apart from your spouse

All such "strings" have to be cut if we are to keep our marriage structure sound.

CLEAVE TO THE COVENANT

Reciting a Covenant with Each Other and God

Leaving is important. But as important as leaving is, it's only a first step. Marriage is a two-step dance, and cleaving is the second step. With that in mind, let's look at some important things to which we should "cleave."

First, we cleave to the covenant of marriage. When a couple stands before me at the altar, I always say something like this: "Do you promise to love and cherish, to honor or sustain in sickness as in health, in poverty as in wealth, in the bad that may darken your days and in the good that may lighten your ways? Do you so promise, so help you God?"

I've yet to perform a wedding in which a bride or groom has answered, "I don't!" A few have taken a while to get it out, but they always answer, "I do!" And they truly believe with all their hearts they will keep these vows.

What happens at this "I do" moment? In exchanging vows, the man and woman seal a covenant with one another and with God. It's as if they sit down at a table with God to convince Him and their family and friends that they want to spend their lives together—exclusively. And Jesus Christ puts His arm around the couple and says, "Yes." God the Father witnesses the transaction and a sacred covenant is established. The Lord Jesus pronounces the benediction: "What therefore God has joined together, let no man separate" (Matthew 19:6).

Do you remember our triangle illustration about the marriage covenant? God is at the apex, with the husband and wife at their respective corners on the base. As the marriage partners grow closer to God, they actually grow closer to one another. The result of such a covenant relationship is a fulfilling and dynamic marriage.

Many choose to marry in a civil ceremony, before a judge or justice of the peace. In that regard I always think of the old guy who said, "Yeah, I got married at a justice of the peace, and my wedding day is the last time I saw either one of them—justice or peace!"

Contrasting a Covenant with a Contract

Whether you got married in a Christian church, at a justice of the peace, or at a quickie wedding chapel in Las Vegas, you still have taken part in a covenant agreement laid out by God in which He told us to "leave and cleave."

Marriage is a covenant, not a contract. In a morally and socially chaotic world where half of new marriages shatter through divorce, prenuptial agreements—a contractual arrangement—have become increasingly in vogue. Arlene Dubin, a New York divorce lawyer, says that some 20 percent of couples engaged for marriage seek prenuptial agreements.[2]

Consider the stark contrasts between a marriage covenant and a contract.

COVENANT	CONTRACT
Based on love	Motivated by commitment
Based on law	Motivated by compulsion
Assumes relationship "till death us do part"	Prepares for marriage to fail
"What's mine is yours"	Protects what is "mine"
"Your interests are my interests"	Secures "my" interests
Prepares for life together	Prepares for life apart

Couples seeking contractual agreements seem to expect that someone or something will separate what God has joined together. They appear to see such an agreement as an easy way to open the "back door" for a swift and clean getaway.

If you choose to operate your marriage only as a legal contract, you may stay together, you may even love one another deeply—but all you will have is you, your mate, and the state! You will miss the dynamic relationship that comes only with the spiritual bonding and intimacy of a divine covenant. God's formula, and only His formula, gives significance, creativity, and sizzle to a marriage.

Cleave to the sacred reality of the marriage covenant! And understand that what God joins together, no man or no thing is to drive apart.

CLEAVE TO GOD'S PRINCIPLES

Apply His "True" Truth

The Bible is our manual for every phase of life, including marriage. It gives us instruction for every important aspect of marriage—whom to marry, how to maintain and grow a strong and healthy marriage, and how to help and heal a hurting marriage.

The single biblical principle we've been exploring in this chapter (leaving and cleaving) is enough to get a couple through any kind of crisis. But the Bible contains additional wisdom on how to handle everything from the smallest conflicts to the most major crises. Even if the marriage gets fragmented, we can give the pieces to God, apply the principles shown in Scripture, and watch Him do a supernatural work of restoration.

Every one of the ten marriage commandments in this book is rooted in *the principles of God,* His "true Truth." The key to using God's principles in your marriage is to make sure you don't just read about them but that you apply them to every facet of your marriage.

Watch Out for a "Sensual Song"

Unfortunately, too many of us are like the people about whom God warned Ezekiel. The prophet taught the people of his day God's principles of life. The members of the crowd turned to one another and said, "Let's go hear the message coming from the Lord!" But God told Ezekiel what was really happening:

> They come to you as people come, and sit before you as My people and hear your words, but they do not do them, for they do the lustful desires expressed by their mouth, and their heart goes after their gain. Behold, you are to them like a sensual song by one who has a beautiful voice and plays well on an instrument; for they hear your words but they do not practice them. So when it comes to pass—as surely it will—then they will know that a prophet has been in their midst. (Ezekiel 33:31–33)

God gives us the same alert today. Though some may congratulate the pastor on his sermon and even invite people to church with them, for many it's as if they've heard a "sensual song." They feel entertained but do not take the principles they heard into the core of their lives and put them into practice.

Don't make such a mistake in your marriage. Hear God's principles, make sure you understand them, put them into practice—and reap the delightful relationship that God wants you to enjoy.

CLEAVE TO YOUR MATE

My earlier "super glue" illustration might have led some readers to think that cleaving means a husband and wife must become inseparable. But that's not what cleaving means. Husbands and wives don't have to be together physically all the time. How would such a thing even be possible? But they do need to be together in their hearts.

Sound "corny"? Maybe it is. Nevertheless, I can say that Jo Beth is always in my heart and that I'm always in hers. What is important to her is important to me. What troubles me, troubles her. When she's insulted, I'm insulted. When I'm hurt, she's hurt. We strengthen each other, we encourage each other, we hold each other. In other words, we cleave, in both good times and in bad. We are covenant partners. And just as Eve completed Adam, Jo Beth completes me.

What happens when we leave our parents and the people, problems, and places of our past, and we cleave to the sacred covenant of marriage, the principles of God, and our mates? The answer is *unity*—we are one flesh!

TWO BECOME ONE

Years ago, when I lived in the mountains of North Carolina, some men in my church talked me into a bear-hunting trip. After climbing to the top of a bluff, I got myself all situated and began praying that a bear *wouldn't* show up!

Ah, but the view from where I sat was worth it. I could look down and see two streams coming together to form a beautiful river. One of the streams carried quite a bit of debris from the mountain as a result of melting snow. The other seemed somewhat silty. So I sat and watched as these little creeks flowed along quietly . . . until they met one another. At the point of convergence, these two trickling streams became churning white water!

No more peaceful, babbling brooks, but loud, roaring rapids. Each stream brought all the debris that had come down with it from farther up the mountain. As I looked beyond those rapids to where the two had become a single waterway, I saw they had become clear, clean, and quiet. They seemed to flow in harmony.

So it is in marriage. When two people become one, there may be an explosive convergence as they adjust to the new relationship. But as they get farther "downstream," a wonderful thing happens: oneness.

If we are to have this oneness in our marriages, we must do everything we can to cleave to our mates physically, emotionally, and spiritually. We're wise if we do it just the way God planned it when He said, "For this cause shall a man leave his father and his mother, and shall cleave to his wife; and they shall become one flesh." That's God's picture of true unity within a marriage. And as we walk in His principle of leaving and cleaving, we will fulfill the promise of oneness.

It works every time.

REFLECTING ON YOUR RELATIONSHIP

If you are married:

1. On whom did you depend most before you married?
2. How has marriage affected that prior relationship?
3. Describe the greatest bond between you and your spouse.

4. What specific things do you need to "leave" in order to intensify the bond between you and your spouse?

If you are contemplating or preparing for marriage:

1. On whom do you most depend right now?
2. How will that relationship change once you are married?
3. Describe several areas of your lives where you and your beloved have grown together during courtship.
4. What things do you need to leave behind as you prepare for marriage?

going out on outings, dinner movies, Conversation

friends, family

A PERSONAL WORD
Thou Shalt Continually Communicate

(Tommy)

Men, *I wrote this chapter with you especially in mind. Females are "Phi Beta Kappa" at communication (usually), while we males tend to be the strong, silent type (or at least pretend to be). Let your wife know what's going on in your life. This commandment plays a big part in making your partner your closest friend. The bottom line is—learn to communicate!*

—E. Y.

Commandment 3

THOU SHALT CONTINUALLY COMMUNICATE

Just a few days after beginning their honeymoon, Rob and Anne had a sharp disagreement. Anne shut down and rebuffed all of Rob's attempts to discuss the problem. Every time he tried to get her to open up, she would reply curtly, "Everything is fine."

Finally, in a calm manner, Rob told his new bride their marriage simply could not function like this. After some discussion, Anne and Rob agreed to a hard and fast rule: They would never use the silent treatment on each other. They agreed that while times would come when they would have to postpone debate in order to cool down, under no circumstances would they ever use silence as a weapon. Then and there they made open communication a priority.

Rob and Anne remained faithful to that commitment and, as a result, have enjoyed more than three decades of happy marriage. Over the years Anne has told many friends how much she appreciated Rob taking the initiative at the very beginning of their married life to insist on honest and open communication.

THE CRITICAL FACTOR

People give all kinds of reasons why they believe a certain marriage will work out:

- "They have so much in common."
- "They are both from such good families."
- "They are both such solid Christian people."

Now, all of these are great reasons and certainly can contribute to a couple's success. But I strongly believe that one factor above all others can make or break a marriage. If a couple makes this area a priority, they likely will enjoy an intimate and meaningful relationship for life. If they neglect it, chances are they'll wind up in a miserable union—if the marriage lasts at all. What's the single factor? *Communication.*

Talk to any number of happily married couples, and you'll find one common thread: good communication. On the other hand, if you were to survey an average group of divorced men and women, more than likely you'd discover that a breakdown in communication lies at the heart of most marital split-ups. Certainly you'd hear of infidelity and irreconcilable differences and an assortment of other reasons. But in most cases, with a little probing, you would discover these reasons all stem from a core problem: poor communication.

If you could sit with me as I listen to couples who have suffered through prolonged marital unhappiness or divorce, you would hear these or similar questions:

"When did we stop communicating?"

"Why don't we talk anymore the way we used to?"

"Where did we go wrong?"

Too many couples unconsciously buy into the idea that when they say, "I do," live under the same roof, eat from the same table, and sleep in the same bed, they automatically grow in intimacy. Yet the simple fact is that if those two people are not communicating—if they are merely occupying adjoining space—they are not growing together but growing apart. Good communication between a husband and a wife takes time and effort. And it's so critically important that I've made it the third commandment of marriage: *Thou shalt continually communicate.*

UNDERSTANDING MARITAL COMMUNICATION

Because many of us don't understand the fundamentals of good communication, it's no wonder we feel "hamstrung" in establishing and maintaining it in our homes. Most of us would probably define communication as "the conveying of information through the use of words." In other words, if two people are talking, they are communicating.

Good communication, of course, does require the use of words. But there is much more to it than that.

Nonverbal factors such as tone of voice, facial expressions, and body language can affect communication far more than one's choice of words. Suppose I were to say, in a sincere tone of voice delivered from a friendly posture, "You're the nicest person I've met in a long time." You rightly would interpret my words as my honest opinion. But what if I were to deliver that same statement while changing my tone of voice and posture and injecting a little sarcasm? In that case I would convey a completely different message. I'd be saying, in effect, "I haven't met any nice people for a long time, and you're the 'least nice' of all the people I've met!"

Since communication is far more than the verbal delivery of information, establishing effective dialogue can be a complex and challenging task. So let's first look at what hinders good communication. Then we'll consider some principles for effective, meaningful communication.

HINDRANCES TO GOOD COMMUNICATION

Let's begin at the beginning . . . back in the Garden of Eden. Things have never been the same since Adam and Eve plunged headlong into sin.

To prompt the "Fall," the serpent used negative communication, namely, deception (Genesis 3:1, 4–5). He used a rhetorical question—"Indeed, has God said 'You shall not eat . . .'?" —to try to deceive Eve; he twisted God's words to imply God was depriving her of all fruit; and he plain lied about the outcome and God's motives. After Eve had been duped into eating the forbidden fruit, she encouraged Adam to try it. Half-truths, manipulation, and downright dishonesty have become tools of communication between men and women ever since!

To improve communication, a couple needs to consider the obstacles blocking it. Any number of activities or commitments can consume a couple's time and energy and keep them from communicating fully and deeply. Even the most positive and worthwhile things can drain away precious time and energy.

Schedules

One recent poll indicated that 61 percent of Americans would trade money for more time.[1] Tragically, many husbands and wives have traded their marriages for their schedules.

Certainly we live in a busy world that never seems to slow down. If anything, it gets busier. Work, appointments, errands, recreation, children, extended families—all these and more contribute to the communication vacuum between husbands and wives.

Many marriages appear happy and healthy, simply because

the husband and wife have so much going on. But a couple can quickly find themselves out of time, out of energy, and drained of emotion—and anything more than the most basic communication can seem all but impossible.

Healthy communication cannot occur and flourish in a marriage in which the partners fail to take time away from all the busyness to be with each other. And if they can't build communication, they can't build their marriage.

Children

While children certainly are the most important result of intimacy in marriage, they can also be the biggest hindrance to it! Children bring great blessings to a marriage, yet they also bring huge responsibilities, perhaps the biggest responsibilities God entrusts to couples. Parents provide the primary source of support for these little human beings for the better part of two decades and possibly longer. Beyond all doubt children make it more difficult for husbands and wives to make time for intimacy and communication.

There is no more demanding creature on planet Earth than a baby. Just ask any new parent. My son Cliff and his wife, Danielle, just had their second little girl. Let me tell you, taking care of Susannah is a full-time job! They have to feed her, change her diapers, bathe her, give her affection—often in the middle of the night. And in between, they're caring for their two-year-old, Rachel. Even as Susannah grows and matures, she will require an extraordinary amount of attention; only the *kind* of attention will change, not the amount.

As babies, children need constant care; as toddlers and preschoolers, they need help to develop the ability to talk and read and interact socially. During the elementary school years, children need emotional and educational support. And when the adolescent years roll around, parents must provide untold hours and endless varieties of support and advice.

Good parents know that when a hungry baby cries, they can't say, "Not now; I'm sleeping!" When their fourth grader asks for help with a math problem, good parents would never shove him aside and say, "Figure it out yourself!" And parents should not miss the opportunity to communicate with their teenagers when they want to talk about personal conflicts at school or dating relationships. When a child genuinely needs attention—and they *very* frequently do—a good parent will always choose to give that attention in every way necessary.

All this takes time away from your spouse. Indeed, the attention your children require can lead to their becoming the center of your life—to the exclusion of marital communication and intimacy.

Finally, when the last child leaves home—and eventually they do—the "empty nest syndrome" sets in. A husband and wife are left with whatever relationship they built between one another while the children lived at home. I've seen it time and time again—couples with nothing to talk about, nothing to share. Without major work, such a marriage can land in serious trouble.

Television

I hit a nerve every time I describe this third obstacle to communication. It's amazing, even alarming, how many people cannot seem to function without television.

Stephen Seplow and Jonathan Storm, writing in *The Philadelphia Inquirer,* reported "about 40% of all the hours not committed to working, eating, sleeping or doing chores" is consumed by TV viewing for many Americans. They noted that by the time the average American dies, he or she will have spent a *decade* in front of a television set![2] Like it or not, since its arrival on the scene some fifty years ago, television has taken a central place in our culture.

Now, don't jump to conclusions—I, too, watch television.

I can think of many positives about TV. It provides a "window" to the world and serves as an educational tool. And there's nothing wrong with a little entertainment from time to time. But when TV becomes a mind-numbing escape or interferes with our relationships, it crosses the line into a destructive addiction.

Who knows how many Americans have become addicted to television? Hundreds of thousands? Millions? Could you be one of them? To find out, try an experiment: Turn off your set for a week. If you're used to coming home, plopping into a recliner with a dinner tray on your lap, and grabbing the remote for a quiet getaway of "channel surfing," then I predict you'll have a tough time turning off the TV. But do it anyway. And then take a walk with your husband or wife and talk about anything and everything.

Fear of Conflict

If a husband and wife never have any conflicts, they probably aren't communicating. Conflict is part of any normal marriage. As long as both partners remain willing and able to communicate, they can overcome conflict and even grow and learn from it. But some people allow their fear of conflict to keep them from effectively communicating with anyone, including their spouse.

Suppose a man grew up in a home where his parents settled conflicts or disagreements according to volume: Whoever yelled the loudest or broke the most dishes won. Such a man might feel afraid to truly communicate, since he associates disagreements with loud or violent outbursts. Or perhaps a woman grew up in a home in which her mother was constantly belittled by verbal put-downs or sarcasm. In her own marriage, such a woman might hesitate to express her thoughts or feelings for fear of being hurt or humiliated.

Schedules, children, television, and fear of conflict are

merely four of the most common obstacles facing couples who want effective communication in their marriages. If they are to create solid and happy homes, however, husbands and wives must find ways to overcome these hindrances. Successful marriages clear away the obstacles and labor to build layer upon layer of effective communication.

LEVELS OF COMMUNICATION

Dr. David Mace, a pioneer in the field of marriage enrichment, wrote several books on improving marriages and marriage communication. In 1973 he and his wife, Vera, founded the Association for Couples in Marriage Enrichment (ACME) with the slogan, "To work for better marriages, beginning with our own."

The Maces stressed a commitment to growth, the ability to make creative use of conflict, and an effectively functioning communication system as the keys to a happy union. ACME insists that "couples must have a mutually agreed upon system of talking with and listening to each other. Since all communication is learned, what is not helpful can be unlearned and new skills substituted for those that hinder the relationship."[3]

Throughout his work, Mace emphasized "deep communication" between a husband and wife. He and other marriage counselors have noted there are various levels at which spouses try to talk to one another.[4] Sadly, most communicate on level one, the shallowest level of all—that of simply exchanging clichés. Let's examine each level of communication.

1. Clichés

"How's it going?"

"How are you today?"

I've discovered that when someone greets me with one of these clichés, he really isn't asking for a report on how things are going. One time, I actually stopped the person and began answering the question in detail. You should have seen the shock on his face as he began backing away, making excuses that he was late for a meeting. Now, I don't recommend you doing this! It could lead to an embarrassing situation. But for sake of illustration, I just had to see that if what I thought would happen, really would. And it did.

When someone asks, "How are you?" he doesn't especially want to know your physical, emotional, or spiritual condition. He is simply trying to be polite by greeting you in a socially acceptable way.

Clichés and casual conversation serve to acknowledge someone's presence; they have little to no essential meaning. We use them in casual contact, with business associates, and with new acquaintances. They mean little more than does a simple handshake.

Even the most damaged marriages move beyond this most elemental level of communication, as do our most casual friendships.

2. Just the Facts

One level up from clichés comes the delivery of factual information. At this level, we communicate facts apart from any kind of interpretation or opinion or emotional response.

"It's raining today."

"The meeting is scheduled for 1:00 P.M."

"It's time to change the oil in the car."

Every healthy relationship requires the exchange of facts. The communication of facts helps a married couple to plan everything from what they will wear or do on a particular day to how they will care for one another and their children.

While husbands and wives certainly need to learn how to accurately communicate facts, they can hardly sustain and grow a healthy marriage on this alone. A healthy personal

71

relationship of any kind requires both parties to communicate on a still deeper level.

3. Opinions and Convictions

When we communicate an opinion, we begin to give the hearer a glimpse of what makes us tick. In other words, the person discovers not just what we think but why. Our statements of opinion or conviction reflect our beliefs, loyalties, and personal commitments. By communicating an opinion or conviction, we state a fact and what we believe about that fact. Most often we communicate opinions or convictions by beginning with statements such as:

"I believe that . . ."
"I think that . . ."
"It appears to me that . . ."

If you were talking with your spouse about a shake-up at the office, the facts might sound like this: "They moved Bill over to accounting and then promoted Frances to take his old position." But you might also communicate your opinion by saying, "I think that change is going to make for a smoother-running office, once we get used to working with Frances," or, "They shouldn't have treated Bill that way."

It's at this level of communication that conflicts often arise. When married couples begin to share opinions and convictions, disagreements can develop, which can escalate into arguments. Yet this is not necessarily a bad or unhealthy thing, so long as both sides respect one another and remain willing to work out their disagreements in love.

4. Feelings

"What are you feeling?"

This question causes most men to break out into a sweat! It seems that we men often struggle at this level. We're great at communicating facts. We're not too bad at voicing our opinions. But most of us labor at sharing our feelings.

We *know* facts, we *believe* our opinions, but we *experience* our feelings—and some of us have lost touch with that experience. Imagine if you were telling your spouse about that "office shake-up." Your feelings toward Bill's replacement could be relief, joy, anger, or disappointment. You might even feel betrayed. It all depends on your opinions and personal feelings toward Bill or toward the preshake-up work situation. Would you be able to describe your feelings to your spouse?

At the feelings level, we enter something of a "danger zone" in our relationships. Here's why: Communicating feelings requires making ourselves vulnerable. We let our spouses know that we feel happy, anxious, upset, or angry—and sometimes at *them!* Discovering what's really going on in the heart of a husband or wife frightens many married people.

Yet to grow in our marriages, we have to grow in our communication. And to grow in our communication, we must learn to communicate our feelings—freely, but with wisdom.

5. Communicating Needs

We reach the deepest level of communication when we communicate our needs. Any marriage counselor, Christian or secular, will insist on the crucial place in the human psyche of communicating needs. Married couples especially have to learn how to communicate at this level.

Fortunately, we communicate our needs almost instinctively, beginning as infants. Babies cry when they feel hungry, need changing, or just want to be picked up. As we mature, we learn to verbalize our needs more articulately: "Mom, I'm hungry!" As we grow into adulthood, our needs become more complex, as do our ways of communicating those needs.

In marriage, both husband and wife must learn to tactfully but directly communicate their needs. This is where the all-important "give-and-take" must occur. Both the husband and wife must learn to communicate their need for affection, for quiet time, for "solitary" time, for conversation, for encouragement, and for all the other needs God intends to provide through marriage. It is within the framework of this level of communication that a couple bonds and blends and become one.

MARRIAGE MEANS
COMMUNICATING WITH A FOREIGNER

John Gray's best-selling *Men Are from Mars, Women Are from Venus* shocked the world with the not especially keen observation that men and women think and react differently to the same situations.

Imagine that! Men think differently than women. It bothers some segments of our population that God wired men and women differently, but you don't have to be married long to realize that huge differences exist in the way men and women think and communicate. While I wouldn't say that men and women are from different planets, I will acknowledge that the sexes seem at least to hail from foreign nations.

Just as problems can arise when people from different countries try to communicate, so can problems arise when men and women try to communicate—*if* they don't put in the effort necessary to truly understand one another.

The word *foreigner* suggests someone who talks differently, perhaps thinks differently, and has a different cultural background from my own. A man from Malaysia is different from me; yet that doesn't make him all wrong, any more than it makes me all right. We're simply different.

That's how it is with my wife and me. If I looked at Jo Beth from a completely "Edwin" perspective, I'd conclude that she is wired all wrong. Not only does she look completely different from me, she also thinks, reasons, and communicates in a completely foreign way. Yet after more than four decades of marriage, I can now celebrate my differences with Jo Beth. I thank God that we balance one another out. She's strong where I'm weak, and I'm strong where she's weak. It hasn't always been easy for us to learn to communicate effectively with the "foreigner" we each married, but it has been well worth the effort.

So how do you communicate with a foreigner? Here are two simple steps to help you better communicate with the "foreigner" to whom you're married.

Talking—and Listening—Straight

The first step may seem obvious, but many married couples struggle with it. Say what you mean! Only one person can control how you communicate, and that person is you. Many couples struggle to communicate effectively because they avoid straight talk. They don't say what they mean, what they need, and what they want.

Many people find such straight talk uncomfortable, even frightening. They fear to communicate exactly what they need and want, so they drop hints (that often go unrecognized). Others go too far with "straight talk," issuing their demands with little tact or sensitivity. Still others try the most dysfunctional forms of communication, such as outbursts of anger or the dreaded "silent treatment." But nothing beats good, honest, open communication.

Years ago Jo Beth and I were on a road trip. She spotted an exit and said, "Would you like to stop and get something to drink?" I completely missed what she intended to communicate and so replied, "No, I'm OK. Let's just press on."

A half hour later, as we approached another exit, Jo Beth said explicitly what she hinted at earlier. "I sure would like to stop and get something to drink," she announced.

"Why didn't you tell me earlier?" I asked.

"I asked you if you wanted something to drink, so I thought you would ask me."

In Jo Beth's mind, "Would you like to stop and get something to drink?" meant, "I would like to stop and get something to drink." But that's not how I heard it. In my mind, my wife asked a straightforward question and I replied with a straightforward answer: "No, I'm fine."

In one way, my wife's question reflected an unselfish approach. She had no intention of manipulating my response. She wanted something to drink, so she threw out her question, hoping I'd respond, "Why, yes, honey, I am thirsty. I think I would like to stop for a Coke."

Since those days, however, Jo Beth has learned that she'll get much further with me by being direct and to the point, while I've learned to listen more intently when she throws out her "suggestions."

Do you want or need something from your mate? Then it's up to you to tell him or her what you want. Dropping hints might be fine for Christmas shopping, but regular, day-to-day communication demands a more direct approach.

Say what you mean and mean what you say—but do so with tact and sensitivity. I always feel a little leery of those who say, "I always say what I mean. You never have to guess with me." People like that often move beyond directness and head toward cruelty or even abuse. I have known married couples whose overly direct communication has devastated their marriages.

Speaking forthrightly, however, makes up only one-half of "straight talk." Listening actively makes up the other half. The only way we'll ever get the whole picture is by concentrating on the words, as well as searching for other clues, such as verbal nuances, facial expressions, and body language.

Listening is hard work! It means listening with the ears, watching with the eyes, and understanding how your spouse acts and reacts—and you cannot achieve straightforward communication without it.

Learning How Your Spouse Is "Wired"

The second step is to understand how your spouse is "wired." How does your spouse best give and receive messages? This means deciphering if he or she is an auditory person, a visual person, or a "feeling" person.

Auditory people like to communicate verbally. They use words carefully and take great pains to analyze how others use them. The auditory person wants and needs to *hear* how much he or she is loved. If your husband or wife falls into this category, then you need to frequently *speak* the words "I love you." Nothing else can replace the *sound* of those precious words.

The *visual* person paints a mental picture of an idea and communicates most effectively on a visual level. This individual may love to hear the words "I love you," but he or she wants to *see* those words demonstrated in loving actions. By and large, we men are visual creatures.

The *feelings* person accurately perceives messages even when little or no visual or verbal communication seems to be occurring. The feelings individual picks up moods, demeanor, and posture. This person senses what others communicate nonverbally, and likely communicates in the same way.

A good car salesman can demonstrate the benefits of knowing and responding to a person's communication wiring. A successful car salesman almost instinctively picks up on what potential car buyers want when they walk through the showroom door. Such a salesman may not consciously think of it this way, but in order to effectively sell his cars, he needs to know how his customer is wired—visual, auditory, or feelings.

The salesman might steer the visual customer toward a sleek, flashy vehicle. He'll be quick to point out how sharp the car looks and how great the customer looks behind the wheel. You can be sure he'll point out the aesthetics of the car's interior—the colors, the appearance of the dashboard, the rich leather upholstery. The visual person might be tempted to purchase such a car simply because of the way it looks.

X The auditory car buyer, on the other hand, listens to the car—how the engine runs, how the transmission shifts, what the doors sound like when they slam shut, how well the interior muffles noise when the car is moving, how well the entertainment system plays a favorite CD. This individual will not buy the car if it doesn't "sound" right.

The feelings customer pays most attention to the "image" of an automobile. Carmakers aim most of their advertisements at these individuals; the majority of television ads these days appeal to emotion. They try to elicit feelings within the potential car buyer—and many of them enjoy great success.

The successful car salesman has learned to identify the various kinds of communicators who walk into his showroom. Have you taken the time to identify what kind of communicator your spouse is—how he or she is "wired"? When you do so, you are well on your way to establishing more meaningful, deeper, and healthier marital communication.

JUMP-STARTING
COMMUNICATION IN YOUR MARRIAGE

Another way to deepen marital communication is to be sure your spouse knows how deeply you love and appreciate him or her. God created all of us to respond to words and actions of love and adoration.

Just think of how many times in the Bible God speaks of His love for you and me. We are valuable to Him and He delights in us. God showers us with affection and repeatedly proclaims His personal devotion to us as His children. Therefore, thoughts of God drive me toward Him and make me want to communicate with Him as my Father in heaven.

In a similar way, husbands and wives must make it a priority to speak words of affirmation and love to one another. Such heartfelt words can provide the basis for a whole new level of communication.

A man the Bible identifies as King Lemuel once wrote of a faithful wife: "Her children rise up and bless her; her husband also, and he praises her, saying: 'Many daughters have done nobly, but you excel them all'" (Proverbs 31:28). Lemuel wanted his wife to know that although he could have chosen his mate from a large pool of fine, noble women, he chose *her*—and he got the cream of the crop.

How would you respond if your spouse spoke such affirming words to you? If you knew your spouse loved you enough to brag on you to others, wouldn't you feel more than willing to communicate openly and honestly in your marriage? Nothing creates more fertile ground for great communication in marriage than lavishing your mate with praise and affirmation.

But how do we do this? How do we affirm and build up our mates and give them the kind of approval each of us so desperately desires?

PRAISE IS A MANY SPLENDORED THING

Most of us know how to give verbal praise (even if we don't give it as often as we should). But don't forget the countless nonverbal ways to affirm your spouse!

Nonverbal praise might include your body language, the way you look at your mate, your gestures. A smile or a loving look can do wonders in reassuring your spouse of your genuine love. And imagine what further lines of communication might be opened!

Get creative in your praise; it's really not so difficult. Leave love notes around the house for your husband or wife to find. Jo Beth is "Phi Beta Kappa" at this! I'm forever finding notes on the bathroom mirror, in a sock drawer, or in my golf bag. Nothing elaborate, just a few words expressing her love and appreciation for me—and I love finding them. They tend to crop up when I most need encouragement. It's her way of praising me and communicating her love for me.

I also recommend strategically "spreading good reports" about your husband or wife. When you say good things about him or her to a friend or relative, your words of affirmation will more than likely make it back to their ears. And when that happens, your mate will know what an important place he or she has in your heart.

One important note on communicating praise: always make sure it's genuine. Be certain that you're acting to build up your spouse and to open fresh lines of communication. Don't let selfish motives find their way into your praise. And avoid flattery; don't speak insincere words of praise in order to gain some personal benefit.

What can happen when we begin to pour praise into the life of our marriage partner? Years ago I read of praise's power in a newspaper column written by a marriage counselor, who I'll call Dr. Crane.

Dr. Crane reported that an angry woman came in to see him one day. "My husband has so hurt me," she fumed. "I want not only to divorce him; I want *revenge.* I want to hurt him. I want to destroy him."

Dr. Crane's advice probably surprised the woman. "Go home and act as if you really love him. Praise him, honor him, build him up. Cook his favorite meals. Employ all the creative chemistry that you can find in your lovemaking arsenal. Tell him that you just can't resist him, that everything about him is supercolossal and fabulous. Play it as if you're madly, help- lessly in love with him. Tell him that he is your hero and your champion, that he's everything to you."

He told the wife to give herself unreservedly to her husband. Once she did that—had truly captivated him with her attention and convinced him that she was just crazy about him—"Then hit him with both barrels. Tell him, 'I hate you! I have the meanest lawyer in town and we're going to skin you alive. You won't have a penny to your name when I'm through with you.'"

"Do that," Dr. Crane finished, "and he'll spend the rest of his life in absolute misery, because he'll never find anybody to match up with you."

"That's it!" the woman cried. "That's what I'm going to do!"

So she went home and acted as if she really loved her husband. Dr. Crane didn't hear from the woman for about three months. Finally he called her and asked, "Are you ready for the divorce?"

"*Divorce?*" she replied. "I'm married to the most wonderful man on the face of this earth! Why would I want a divorce?"

That is what can happen when we begin praising our mates in both words and actions. Severed lines of communication can be repaired and function once more. And even the most difficult marriage can become the loving, supportive institution God meant it to be.

AN "EIGHT-COW" WIFE

Years ago I read an article about an American who visited a group of South Pacific islands.[5] Everywhere the man went, he would hear the islanders talking about a fellow named Johnny Lingo. Whatever he wanted to do, from going fishing to buying pearls, the people would tell him that Johnny Lingo was the man to see. It seemed that whatever his question, "Johnny Lingo" was the answer!

He did notice one odd thing, though. While the islanders would brag on Johnny Lingo and describe his talents, they'd also chuckle among themselves and give each other a wink. After a while the visitor began to wonder: *If he's such a wonderful person, then what's the joke?* Yet no one would divulge the secret.

Finally, a local man decided to give the writer the "inside scoop" on the island's favorite son, Johnny Lingo. The custom among Johnny's people was for a suitor to "buy" a wife by offering the father cows in payment. One or two cows might buy a plain wife, but a "five-cow wife" was a real beauty.

Johnny was rich, the man said, but he had paid eight cows for his wife—much too much. Sarita, the bride, was "plain," the man explained. "She was skinny and walked with hunched shoulders and bowed head. She was scared of her own shadow." He grinned, then told the American, "We've never been able to figure out how Johnny Lingo, the sharpest trader on the island, somehow was tricked into paying her father, old Sam Karoo, eight cows for a one- or two-cow bride."

The story so intrigued the visitor that he made an appointment to visit Johnny Lingo in person. When they met, Johnny showed his guest great hospitality. They talked awhile before the guest asked about the unusually high payment for Johnny's wife. "Always and forever," Johnny replied, "when they speak of marriage settlements it will be remembered that Johnny Lingo paid eight cows for Sarita.

Just then, a stunningly beautiful woman walked into the little hut—the most gorgeous woman the writer had ever seen. Every inch of her striking frame exuded loveliness: the tilt of her head, the confident way she walked, her smile, and her radiance.

Johnny looked at his puzzled visitor. Then he said: "Many things can change a woman. Things that happen inside, things that happen outside. But the thing that matters most is what she thinks about herself. In Kiniwata, Sarita believed she was worth nothing. Now she knows she is worth more than any other woman in the islands."[6]

Johnny communicated to everyone in the islands, loud

and clear, that he loved Sarita and felt proud to make her his bride. He proves that sparkling communication, through loving words and actions, can achieve what nothing else can. It works in the islands, and it can work in your home too.

REFLECTING ON YOUR RELATIONSHIP

1. On a scale of 1 to 10 (1 being nonexistent and 10 being "so good, no improvement is possible"), rate the communication in your marriage.
2. How are you and your spouse at communicating your feelings and needs to one another?
3. Describe some hindrances to communication in your marriage.
4. How is your spouse wired? Auditory? Visual? Feelings? In light of your spouse's "wiring," how can you best communicate your love to him or her?

A PERSONAL WORD
Thou Shalt Make Conflict Thy Ally

Conflict can destroy a marriage. But it also can bring fresh breezes and new life into the relationship. The marriage can become stronger through disagreements and adversity.

Sometimes marriage is like a duel. When we learn how to successfully handle conflict, guess what? It becomes a duet and the harmony produced from it is almost divine. So decide whether your marriage is going to be a duel or a duet.

—E. Y.

Commandment 4

THOU SHALT MAKE CONFLICT THY ALLY

Surely you and your wife never fight, *do you?* I wish I had a nickel for every person who has asked me that question, and just a penny for all the others who actually believe it. I'd be a wealthy man!

Jo Beth and I have been married more than forty years, so you might think that by now we are through with all the battles and disagreements. Surely after forty years we've got everything worked out! Well, not exactly. Once in a while I have to "remind" Jo Beth of some basic principles. Actually, that's not true—it happens *regularly!* And more often, she has to "remind" me.

I'm grateful that Jo Beth and I have a strong marriage, but as I've admitted throughout this book, we are still growing in our relationship and still have areas to work on. Sometimes we agree; sometimes we don't. No marriage is immune to conflict. Remember, in marriage, two separate individuals have joined to become one, so some friction and tension certainly will take place at the intersection of their union.

TWO MYTHS ABOUT CONFLICT

The fourth commandment for a successful marriage is one that many couples question. It is: *Thou shalt make conflict thy ally.*

The reason couples question this commandment is because of a couple of prevailing marital myths. So, as we begin, let me quickly explode those two myths.

1. Good marriages do not have problems.

Do you ever fight with your husband or wife? Do you quarrel with your mate? If so, congratulations—you have a perfectly normal marriage.

Some people think that two people in love will never suffer any kind of significant conflict. That's simply not true. Every married couple, no matter how well matched or how spiritually mature, *will* have conflict. It's a normal part of marriage. The question is, how do we handle our battles, fights, misunderstandings, disputes, and miscommunications? The right responses to that question will lead to a great relationship.

2. Conflict hurts good marriages.

Conflict does *not* have to hurt a solid marriage. In fact, conflict is an important part of every good marriage. Handled wisely, it can lead to greater intimacy; handled poorly, it can lead to greater isolation. We can't choose whether we will have conflict, only how we will deal with it. So what will you choose: intimacy or isolation?

In many ways, marriage is like two cold porcupines that move closer together for warmth. They *will* have conflict! Of course, if these two porcupines were to stay by themselves, they could avoid all conflict (and they'd also stay cold). For the porcupine union to work, there has to be some negotiation.

Some people think they have a good marriage because they never have any conflict. How do you think they manage that? I'll tell you how—they live independently of one another. "You do your thing, and I'll do mine. We'll get together every once in a while to deal with a few little things, but by and large, we'll pursue separate and independent agendas."

Anyone can avoid conflict by living like a solitary porcupine. But if you desire true intimacy, you have to make decisions together and move together, not in a duel but as a duet. After all, two porcupines that move closer together must learn to relate to one another very carefully, or they will cause one another tremendous pain. Yet it's out of this kind of conflict that real intimacy comes, resulting in a strong marriage.

All marriages, the good ones and the bad ones, have problems. And the difficulties in each type of marriage closely resemble each other. The crucial difference lies in how a good marriage handles conflict. The Bible tells us to "count it all joy" (James 1:2 KJV) when trials and adversities come. Why count it all joy? Because conflict produces endurance, and endurance produces maturity (vv. 2–4).

GOOD AND BAD CONFLICT

I'm always astounded at the number of people I meet who actually believe marriage will fix their lives and make everything just right. Here's a guy who has difficulty with friends, clashes at work, trouble in school, and poor family relationships—but by getting married, he thinks everything will turn out great. Or a girl who thinks that by saying, "I do," her life will turn blissfully happy "till death do us part." Where did we get such a foolish idea?

The Bible tells us that conflict goes all the way back to the Garden of Eden. When sin entered this world, it negatively affected every relationship in every family. Nevertheless, as I've suggested, conflict in marriage is not always sin. The presence of problems, tensions, and arguments doesn't necessarily mean trouble for a marriage.

I believe that Adam and Eve had good conflict *prior* to their sin. I can't imagine Adam sitting there, telling Eve what he had named all the animals, and Eve not having a better idea once in awhile, can you? Two very different personalities, both created by God, are bound to have differences of opinion . . . with conflict ensuing.

But there is both good and bad conflict. There is *constructive* conflict and *destructive* conflict.

Suppose a man has a friend named Jack who has a birthday coming up. He says to his wife, "Honey, let's not forget to send Jack a card. His birthday is next week."

His wife replies, "Jack is one of your best friends. I think you ought to get him a birthday present and not just a card."

"No way," he answers. "Jack wouldn't want a present. We're grown men. A card will be more than adequate."

"But Jack isn't any old friend; he's your *best* friend," she responds. "Remember, he also took you to the ball game last week."

"Well, sure Jack and I are close," he admits, "but anything more than a birthday card just wouldn't fit."

"Listen," she insists. "It's his fortieth birthday and that's a tough time for good old Jack. He's going through a real transition right now. I think if you did a little extra, it would be really nice. Wasn't he there with you when your dad passed away? And he's been at your right hand all these years. So get him a present. I think it'll do him good."

Let's stop the conversation at this point. Here we see a conflict arising out of a difference of opinion, not out of sin. Let's consider three ways such a conflict could be handled.

First, the husband could say, "You know, I think you're

right. Jack *is* special. And it is his fortieth birthday. What do you suggest we get him?"

Second, he could say, "I don't think we need to get Jack anything for his birthday. We're adults, for Pete's sake. But if it'll make you happy, go and buy him something and I'll give it to him."

Third, he could say, "I am absolutely opposed to getting Jack a birthday present; that's just stupid and childish. How ridiculous! And he's *my* friend, not *yours*—so stay out of my life. Now I've got to go. You always bring up such crazy things when I'm in a hurry." And he storms out of the house.

The first scenario demonstrates a constructive response to conflict. The husband ponders his wife's suggestion and thinks, *My wife knows about these things better than I do. She's a birthday person; she remembers all of them.* So he says to her, "I think you're right." His response encourages her to continue to offer advice—and most of us men need advice even if we won't admit it.

The second approach just shuts her down. She gets her way—Jack gets a birthday gift—but the approach does more harm than good, for she receives no encouragement to offer her husband any assistance in the future.

The third response is purely destructive. He banishes her from the battlefield and uses some terminal words to wound her spirit, such as "ridiculous," "stupid," "crazy," and "childish."

John Gottman, a marriage researcher at the University of Washington, has studied conflict in marriage. With his wife, Julie, and research psychologist Sybil Carrere, Gottman developed criteria for predicting whether or not a marriage will survive. Gottman and his team reportedly can make the prediction within three minutes of assessing a couple!

For more than two decades the Gottman team has tracked seven hundred couples and can predict with 91 percent accuracy whether couples will divorce. By listening to how a couple argues, according to the specialists, you can tell if a marriage is going to make it. The evidence revealed that couples must take care how they communicate, especially when they argue and fight.[1]

In our illustration, the husband's third response fell into the destructive category mainly because he attacked the *person,* not the *problem.* Over time, this type of response can be fatal to the marriage relationship.

How can we train ourselves to use the conflicts that inevitably come into every marriage for constructive rather than destructive purposes? Let's begin by considering some of the most important traps to avoid.

THE DON'TS OF CONFLICT

Destructive conflict uses several inappropriate weapons of war to "win" its battles. We would head off a lot of this type of conflict if we'd remember the following seven "don'ts."

1. Don't be ashamed of your anger.

Anyone who wants to be useful in this world will get angry. If you never get angry, I doubt you've developed much as a person. Issues should matter; your opinions and conclusions are important. Just remember, anger is not the issue; how you deal with your anger is.

As we've already noted, many times in marriage, opposites attract. We see in that other person something we don't have but like. Often, those differences are what bring the spark and creativity to the relationship.

But what happens when a prizefighter marries a peacemaker? Here's a guy who grew up in a home that responds to conflict by "bringing out the gloves." When a disagreement arose, his family would lay everything on the table and duke it out. Everybody told everybody else what they really thought —and that usually led to relational black eyes.

His peacemaker wife is different. Every time conflict came to her family, everyone grew deathly quiet. *Shhh! Don't mention it, don't bring it up, and don't talk about it.* Anything to keep peace in the family! So as an adult she runs from any kind of conflict or confrontation. She sweeps it under the rug and refuses to admit it exists.

Now look what happens when they marry. The prizefighter sees a problem and yells, "Let's deal with it!" The peacemaker thinks, *Oh, no, I don't want to deal with it. I'll do anything but that. I don't want to talk about it.* So she withdraws and avoids the problem.

Now, who gets in between the prizefighter and the peacemaker? Far too often, it's that little six- or seven-year-old child.

"Daddy, don't you know Mama doesn't like to fight?"

"I don't care what your mama wants," he growls.

Sometimes Junior takes Dad's side.

"Mama, don't you know that Daddy just wants to talk? You need to talk to him."

"I don't want to talk about it," she says. "I *can't* talk about it."

Soon the child can become a human Ping-Pong ball between Mom and Dad.

Let me take a moment to address the worst thing that sometimes happens in this type of relationship: violence. It shatters the home, especially the children. Homes where exploitation and abuse exist tend to create homes of exploitation and abuse. But there's no place for that, ever! If your home suffers from this type of anger, seek out the help and counsel available in your church or community. And remember, even violent marriages can be healed with the aid of caring individuals and a loving and powerful God.

While we shouldn't hide our anger, there is an appropriate way to express anger that has nothing to do with pushing or shoving or slapping or hitting. Anger is a good thing, not a bad thing. The Bible says, "'In your anger do not sin': Do not let the sun go down while you are still angry" (Ephesians 4:26 NIV).

Of course, one has to be mature to handle anger properly —and that's where so many of us miss the boat. We flare up, get angry, and attack the person instead of the problem.

Arguments in which a husband and a wife honestly express their anger can be therapeutic. When disagreements arise, we need to let our mates know that we love them and that it's time to get on with it and settle the dispute. This can be both good and healthy. So don't be ashamed of your anger.

2. Don't call in heavy artillery or use deadly weapons.

While expressing anger can promote a healthy relationship, remember that you're not in this thing to wipe out your spouse. You don't want complete, unconditional victory. Those who fail to figure this out inflame their conflicts, leading to greater isolation instead of greater intimacy. So leave some room to maneuver.

In Operation Desert Storm, the successful offensive during the 1991 Persian Gulf War, allied forces tried to do a minimum amount of damage while making their point. In that war the American news media introduced us to "smart bombs" that could pinpoint a target and do very little, if any, collateral damage. The allies realized that there is such a thing as overkill.

Sometimes when we get into an argument with our mate, we call in the heavy artillery. But instead of the "smart bombs," we send off the errant and unpredictable "Scud missiles" of the enemy. "I'll leave!" we yell. "We'll get a divorce!" We mimic television couples we've seen go ballistic. The TV husband gets up after saying about three words, then storms out and slams the door. And real husbands think, *Now, that's the manly way to handle conflict!*

No, it's not. It's the cowardly thing to do. We need to stay in the ring, listen carefully, and have the courage to deal head-on with whatever troubles our mate. Anybody can run; cowards do it all the time.

3. Don't air your dirty linen in public.

A few years ago I read about a disastrous wedding reception at the Blue Dolphin Inn in southern California. Right in the middle of the reception, while three hundred guests happily talked and reminisced about the young couple, the bride and groom broke into a violent argument. Eventually the groom grabbed part of the wedding cake and threw it in the face of his bride. Kapow! Immediately food fights and fistfights broke out between the families, friends, and members of the wedding party. Bedlam reigned. By the time the police arrived, the bride and groom had disappeared.

This may be an extreme illustration, but it points out the dangers of airing your dirty linen in public. Don't discuss your private conflicts in front of friends, family, or business associates. Also, don't inappropriately pour out your heart to your friends or your parents or some other confidant. That will hurt your mate and do nothing to help resolve normal marital conflict.

4. Don't paint yourself into a corner.

Too many of us paint ourselves into a corner by our poor choice of words. "If you don't stop," we say, "I'll get a lawyer!" We use big, broad, sweeping statements and threats to control our mate. We reach way back into our "arsenal" and drag up something we've dealt with before and bring it into the battle.

All's *not* fair in love and war! If marriages had referees, they'd blow the whistle or throw the flag on this tactic. Don't paint yourself into a corner. Don't maneuver yourself into a position from which there is no retreat.

5. Don't use the turtle approach.

When a turtle encounters a problem, he climbs into his shell, hunkers down, and stays there. A lot of us become turtle-like in the face of marital conflict. We grow silent.

Of course, a little silence may be good. Sometimes we need to back up and think a minute. Sometimes we need to walk away and say, "Time out; let's have a truce."

But that's not the turtle approach. The turtle approach says, "I'm going to remain silent. I'm not going to say anything until she apologizes," or, "I'm not going to respond until he responds." So the two of you sleep side by side in bed, about six inches apart, doing your best to not even touch one another.

Too many of us refuse to face the little conflicts of marriage. We won't get them out into the light and talk about them. And over time our molehills grow into ominous mountains. So avoid the turtle approach. I've never yet met a turtle with a good marriage.

6. Don't keep a chip on your shoulder.

Some of us handle conflict with a chip on our shoulder. We overstate things. We take a little situation and generalize it and make it sound as if it has been the situation from the very beginning. We act like the wife in the middle of a battle who looked at her husband and said, "You have every characteristic of a dog, except one."

"And which one is that?"

"Loyalty."

Humorous, but way too strong! That's a huge overstatement. But some of us do exactly that when we're angry. We keep the chip on our shoulder and allow ourselves to spin out of control.

7. Don't use sex as a weapon.

Some use sex as a tool of punishment or reward. They might say to their mate, "I'm not going to make love to you until we get things worked out." But when sex becomes a weapon of manipulation, the whole physical relationship degenerates. Many a husband grows angry and depressed because he feels as though he has to earn his wife's affection.

Such a weapon can spark an "arms race." Too many husbands have said, "I'll show you. I'll find love in the arms of another woman." Jesus meant it when He said, "All those who take up the sword shall perish by the sword"(Matthew 26:52).

Take care to heed the "don'ts" of conflict! Failure to do so has started innumerable couples down a heartrending path.

FOUR STAGES OF HEART HURT

When we deal with conflict the wrong way, tension continues to build in the home until we progress through four stages of hurt. Each stage can lead to greater alienation between husband and wife.

1. The Wounded Heart

We all know something about this stage. Our mates have wounded us and we've wounded them. Sometimes it happens intentionally, sometimes unintentionally. If we're sensitive at all, we pick up our mate's signals and know when he or she feels wounded. We know when something's wrong, when things have gotten out of balance. No married person can honestly say, "I've never known anything about the wounded heart."

Ignore the wounded heart long enough, and it turns into something else.

2. The Cold Heart

During the second stage, a husband might recognize his wife's wounded heart and begin to talk to her, but without trying to resolve the conflict. Communication takes place, but it lacks any power to resolve the dispute. Usually such communication sounds overly "nice." The couple may act indifferently toward each other. He's Mr. Cool; she's Mrs. Unflustered. "The conflict doesn't bother me!" As they avoid the issue and any meaningful contact with each other, the cold heart sets in.

3. The Hard Heart

The third stage reflects serious trouble. In the hard-heart stage, you begin to grieve the Holy Spirit. You have trouble praying (see Ephesians 4:30; 1 Peter 3:7). When you're not in a right relationship with your mate, how can you pray? Heaven seems blocked and God seems far away. At the hard-heart stage, you're metallic and tough. As you go through the motions, you begin to wonder if your marriage will last. All kinds of conflict may break loose, but you're so hard and cold and businesslike you really don't care.

And that leads to the fourth, and fatal, stage.

4. The Apathetic Heart

The opposite of love is not hate but apathy. It's indifference, an attitude of "I don't care." Through the years I've counseled many couples. On several occasions I've heard men bitterly declare how much they hated their wives, or vice versa. They'd say they couldn't stand this or they despised that. After letting them talk awhile, I'd say, "You really love her, don't you?" They would always look at me, astonished, and ask, "How could you tell?" Easy. It was because of their anger. There's hope for such a man or woman.

But what about the couple who display nothing but apathy and indifference? He doesn't care; she doesn't care. Love seems gone and the marriage destroyed.

How tragic! And it's even more tragic because the marriage

plummeted to the fourth stage over conflicts that didn't even amount to much.

HOW TO KEEP CONFLICT CONSTRUCTIVE

Let's get very practical. How can we keep the conflict in our marriages *constructive?*

Between conflicts, sit down with your partner and determine the pattern of conflict in your marriage. Again, don't do this while the drums roll and everybody is choosing their weapons. Do it when everything seems relatively calm and peaceful. Say to one another, "Let's sit down and talk. Let's do some preventive maintenance."

During what circumstances or times does conflict tend to surface in your marriage? Identify these areas of tension and discuss what you might be able to do about them.

Consider John and Mary. It seems that every time they go out together, World War III breaks out. She gets exhausted early and wants to go home while the evening is young. He's a slow starter and begins having a good time just about the time she feels dead on her feet.

"Oh, let's go," she says.

"No, let's stay a little longer," he replies.

They go home angry almost every time they go out. What should they do?

In a "neutral" moment, they need to sit down and analyze their patterns. They might decide that on the days they plan to go out for the evening, Mary will rest a little in the afternoon. Second, prior to leaving for any "open-ended" event like a party, they will agree on a time to leave. It won't take long for them to understand that John is not trying to exhaust his wife, nor is Mary trying to squash her husband's fun. They realize their problem relates to varying body metabolisms and different personalities, and so they agree upon a procedure that heads off future conflicts.

How simple! Actually, most of our conflicts in marriage don't get much more complicated than that. We could find workable solutions to our disagreements if we would only sit down and deal reasonably with them.

WHEN THE BATTLE LINES ARE DRAWN

Suppose you've not yet practiced "preventive medicine," and the battle lines already have been drawn. What can you do when conflict explodes? Let me suggest several things.

1. Talk and listen to God.

Pray! Verbalize your conflict to God and listen for His response. So many times in moments of conflict, I begin to pray, "Oh, Lord, change my children. Oh, Lord, change my wife." When I finish my little plea, the answer often comes back: "I intend to, but let's start with your children's father and your wife's husband!"

Before you do anything else, talk—and listen—to God.

2. Try to understand your mate.

You say it's too tough to understand your mate? I really doubt that.

We used to have a paperboy who came every morning at the same time, like clockwork. The whole neighborhood could tell when Greg arrived on the scene, including the dogs. The canine crew seemed to come out of the woodwork. You wouldn't believe the barking, howling, and growling that erupted as they all headed for poor ol' Greg. He would take his papers or sticks or rocks or whatever he could find to beat off the dogs. Morning after morning the same bedlam took place.

One day a new paperboy took over the route. At first, all the dogs rushed out as usual, growling and snapping and trying to get him like they had Greg. But this young man had a different plan. He began to speak to the dogs in a welcoming and friendly way. He knew they were all just pets, not really vicious. He figured out that the dogs sensed a challenge to their turf. He understood they felt frightened and insecure. So he began to pet one of the little "beasts." A week went by, and another canine got in on the petting. Finally, the toughest dog in the neighborhood became his best buddy. From that time on, all those "vicious" dogs would run out with their tails wagging whenever they heard the paperboy coming. They felt overjoyed to see him because they knew he was going to pet them.

Now, surely we're as smart as the average paperboy. We need to understand our mates. What frightens her or agitates him? Just think a moment. Could it be your partner feels insecure or needs a little extra "petting"?

3. Try to understand yourself.

This may be the toughest assignment of all. Most of us are either too easy or too hard on ourselves. Ask yourself, "Why am I on edge today? Why did I say that? Why am I acting like this? What's going on in my life that has caused me to bring the office home with me or take my home to the office?"

Be honest. And if you need help in understanding yourself, that's OK. Others sometimes see what we cannot. That's why the Bible says, "The purposes of a man's heart are deep waters, but a man of understanding draws them out" (Proverbs 20:5 NIV). Find a man (or, if a wife, a woman) of understanding and ask this friend to help you see your strengths and your shortcomings. See if he or she can help you draw out the deep waters of your heart.

4. Talk to your mate.

No relationship can thrive without regular and healthy communication. But when you talk, make sure you pick positive, edifying words.

You know how most men and women respond to conflicts in marriage? They react with harsh words. They retaliate. They offer insult for insult. For instance,

- "Why do you wear your wedding ring on the wrong finger?" a wife asks.

    "Because it reminds me I married the wrong woman," he replies.

- "We have a good marriage," says a wife, "because both of us love the same man—You!"

- "You love football more than you love me," a woman complains.

    "Maybe so," her husband replies, "but I love you better than baseball."

- "What do your husband and you have in common?" a counselor wondered.

    "One thing," the woman replied. "Neither one of us can stand the other."

The statements may be humorous, but they help illustrate the lowest common denominator to which many marriages sink in exchanging insult for insult, injury for injury.

Psalm 141:3 offers a better way. The psalmist asks the Lord to put a watch over his lips. We too need to pray: "Lord, put a watch over my lips; Lord, be the keeper over my mouth." We also could use a dose of Proverbs 15:1, which says, "A gentle answer turns away wrath." We do not return insult for insult, but blessing for insult. We have to learn to trade sweet for bitter. So pick your words carefully.

5. Don't let the sun go down on your anger.

We've said it before: Don't let your wrath fester (see Ephesians 4:26). Don't let your anger get past the wounded heart stage. This doesn't mean you and your spouse agree on everything. It does mean you'll stay up late many nights, making sure you never go to sleep until you get your hearts together.

Jo Beth and I have decided never to go to sleep at night until our hearts get together. The issue may not be resolved, but we will not let anger be our last emotion as we drift off to sleep. We often accomplish this by "touching toes."

Whenever bedtime comes and we're still upset with one another or working through a conflict, we turn out the light and think through the first four steps—talk and listen to God, try to understand your partner, try to understand yourself, and talk to your mate. So as we lie there in the dark, we each pray. We try to understand where the other is coming from, while also looking at ourselves. We think through what's been said and how we've said it. It's amazing how we go through this process at about the same pace.

We finally reach the point where we'll just touch toes in bed. That's our way of saying, "I love you, and I know we're going to work this out."

6. Make confession and forgiveness a priority.

Once you've completed those four steps and "touched toes," the next step is to say, "Honey, I'm sorry. Will you forgive me?" These words allow conflict to open the door to a stronger relationship. So many times offering a little forgiveness is all it takes to bring a couple back together.

In destructive conflict, one individual or another may "win," but the marriage is a loser. Let's learn how to handle conflict in a constructive fashion. When we do, neither individual "wins" but the marriage does. And our relationship grows stronger.

LEARN TO CONTROL YOUR REACTIONS

Have you ever considered that your *reactions* may have a greater effect on your marriage than your *actions?* Actions

101

remain vitally important, of course. We help or hurt those we love with our actions. But even if our actions are perfect, we can devastate our marriages through inappropriate *reactions*.

For example, if I don't lie, cheat, commit adultery, steal, or get drunk, you would say my actions get an A plus. But what if, in a moment of conflict, I lash out with jealousy, hatred, or a spirit of revenge? In a very real sense, my reactions can cause more damage (or create more harmony) than my actions.

Many times, when we react inappropriately, we say, "That really wasn't me. I admit I have a temper, but that was not the real me." I have news for you: that *is* the real me and that *is* the real you. How we respond in a conflict reveals the real person inside.

Think of it this way. What happens when you put a tea bag in a cup of hot water? The water soon begins to turn brown. Why? Did the hot water turn itself brown? No. The "brownness" was in the tea bag the whole time; the hot water merely brought out its natural color.

Or what happens when you squeeze a lemon? Sour, bitter juice comes out. Did the squeezing make the lemon sour and bitter? No. The squeezing merely brought out the sourness and bitterness already present.

In the same way, when we find ourselves in "hot water" or "being squeezed" in our marriages, what comes out is what's inside. Therefore, we need to work not only on our actions toward our mates but also on our reactions in moments of crisis.

"LUCKY FOR HIM . . ."

Conflict comes into every marriage, but it's up to us to make sure it serves a constructive purpose. Conflict in the home can lead to endurance and a deepening of our relationship to both our spouse and to God. And that leads to maturity.

A much-loved grandmother was celebrating her fiftieth

wedding anniversary. One of her daughters asked, "Mama, what is the key to the happiness and joy that you and Daddy have known through the years? Please tell everybody your secret."

"Well," she began, "when your daddy and I first got married, I made a list of ten things I would overlook about his personality—things I just didn't like. The day we walked down the aisle, I made a promise that when any of those ten things came up, I would overlook it for the sake of marital harmony."

"Granny," one of her granddaughters excitedly replied, "please tell us that list. Tell us what those ten things were!"

"Well, honey," she answered, "to be honest, I never did write them down. But every time your grandfather would do something to make me hopping mad, I would think, *Lucky for him it's one of those ten things.*"

What "ten things" make you hopping mad about your own mate? What behavior or event tends to cause the most conflict in your home? Whatever those "ten things" may be, you would be wise to use this grandmother's example—in fact, we all would be. Then we, too, would be on our way to a golden marriage.

REFLECTING ON YOUR RELATIONSHIP

If you are married:

1. How has a conflict resulted in strengthening a weak point in your relationship with your spouse?
2. Are you a peacemaker or a prizefighter? Explain.
3. How do you need to change to make conflict an ally rather than an enemy?
4. How did your parents handle conflict when you were growing up, and how has that pattern affected you?

If you are contemplating or preparing for marriage:

1. What conflicts or tension do you have at present in your relationship? (If you believe there are no conflicts, perhaps you or your beloved are not being open about your attitudes, preferences, or feelings.)
2. Do you express your disagreements to each other? Why or why not?
3. Discuss with your beloved those things that create tensions. Ask him or her to do the same.
4. Together, plan strategies to deal with conflicts in the future.

A PERSONAL WORD
Thou Shalt Avoid the Quicksand of Debt

How you manage finances is simply a question of stewardship—God's ownership, your trusteeship. This chapter tells you how to get out and stay out of debt.

—E. Y.

Commandment 5

THOU SHALT AVOID
THE QUICKSAND OF DEBT

The wedding bells had hardly stopped ringing when a young
South Carolina couple I knew decided they needed a larger
house. Soon these newlyweds leashed themselves to a huge
mortgage payment—but that's not all.

More space to fill meant more furniture and the latest in
technological gadgetry. They also decided their home would
not be complete, nor would it look like all the others in their
subdivision, until a couple of the latest sports utility vehicles
parked in the driveway.

At last, they believed they had achieved the look, the image, and the feel of a successful American couple. And like millions of other such couples, they found themselves sinking in
a quicksand of debt.

One night, while watching their bigger-than-life large-
screen television, they saw a commercial about consolidat-
ing their debt with a home equity loan. They called the number
flashing on the screen and consolidated all the money they

owed into a new "easy payment" loan. Thinking they had magically reduced their debt, they added more payments as they lived increasingly through their charge cards. Before long, this young couple filed for bankruptcy.

With financial stress adding to the woes of their relationship, they began to fight and bicker over money (or its lack). Does it surprise you that they eventually got a divorce?

If you looked at their divorce certificate, probably you would see listed as the reason for the breakup, "incompatibility." That's the word in legalese by which two people declare they can't get along with one another. Whenever I see that word, I'm reminded of a man in Florida who told me straight-out he was divorcing his wife because of "incompatibility." He didn't have enough income and she didn't have enough "pat-ability!"

Income/pat-ability describes well what happens in far too many marriages. Most American divorces result from conflicts over money or sex, and sometimes both. We will consider sex in a later chapter. Let's first look at financial challenges in marriage—especially debt. Thus our fifth marriage commandment: *Thou shalt avoid the quicksand of debt.*

THE TENSIONS MONEY BRINGS

So many tensions in marriage come from the financial realm, though they may find expression in other avenues. Many counselors believe that more than half of all family breakups in America stem from money: too much, not enough, poor management, big bills, interest, and all the rest.

Forty percent of all the wage earners in the United States are women. By some estimates, women control 65 percent of all the wealth in America. In a third of all U.S. households, the wife is the bookkeeper; she pays the bills and controls the pocketbook. That's why credit card hucksters—who send out some two *billion* solicitations a year[1]—target women so aggressively. Ask **any** Christian banker or financier to tell you how much interest you are paying, and it will stagger you!

When MasterCharge changed its name to MasterCard, the company perhaps didn't understand how descriptive the new label really was. That card—and all the others—has "mastered" millions of individuals!

A college girl said to her about-to-be-married best friend, "I certainly hope you have a happy marriage." Her friend replied, "I'm sure we will. We've never had any difficulty in the year we've been going together except in the area of money. And we've agreed when we're married never to talk about money."

In other words, she told her friend, "We'll be happily married until 'debt do us part'!"

A SIMPLISTIC SOLUTION

Many people try to address the money problem with a simplistic solution. They believe if they just had more money, it would solve their problems. The case of one of history's richest men shows the emptiness of that belief. J. Paul Getty was worth more than four billion dollars when he died. Yet Getty, who married five times, reportedly lamented that the only people he envied were those with successful marriages.

The New York Times noted in its obituary of Getty: "Indeed, business was Mr. Getty's life. One of his former wives once remarked, perhaps astringently, that business was his 'first love' and that wealth was merely a byproduct."[2]

How can we learn from Getty's mistakes and build successful marriages? Part of the solution comes in understanding money. Two words help here: *stewardship* and *budget*.

A WORD FOR EVERYDAY LIVING

We should never reserve the term *stewardship* for the stained-glass world. It needs to inform and direct our everyday living.

We misunderstand money and its use when we think of it as all ours, or even as 90 percent ours with 10 percent, the "tithe," going to God. In fact, God owns *everything* and entrusts *some* of it to us to use for a little while. God makes us trustees of His possessions. *Stewardship refers to God's ownership and a human being's partnership.*

Jesus said, "Seek . . . first the kingdom of God and his righteousness; and all these things shall be added unto you" (Matthew 6:33 KJV). When we give first place to the Father's agenda, the Son's priorities, and the causes of God's church, we invest in things that last forever.

Closing the door to the temptation of materialism doesn't depend on how much money you have but how you use it. Changing from an attitude of possessiveness to a worldview of stewardship will slam the door on material temptation.

Families who rethink their priorities can enjoy a remarkable transformation. If husbands and wives would vow that, "Today we are going to readjust, reschedule, replan, reprogram so that we put God's things first," they would build a mighty wall against the temptation of material possessions that can destroy a marriage and family.

10-70-20 BUDGET

A second word, *budget,* can also help to greatly alleviate the problems associated with finances. There are many money-management plans available. Years ago I came across one that I have found particularly useful. It's simple to use and works in most situations, with the possible exceptions of extremely low or high incomes. It's called the "10-70-20 budget."[3] It works like this:

1. First subtract your tithe and your taxes from your gross monthly income. People frequently ask me if they should tithe on their gross or their net income. Re-

member, the Bible teaches that we are to bring to God the "firstfruits," not the "after-tax" fruits, so give from your gross earnings. (And, of course, pay your taxes. The Lord said we are to "Render to Caesar the things that are Caesar's" [Matthew 22:21].)

2. Take 10 percent of what is left after your tithe and taxes and save or invest that amount.
3. Use 70 percent of the remainder for operating essentials.
4. Apply the last 20 percent to debt reduction. (If 20 percent won't cover all the payments, then you may want to consider a debt consolidation loan, but be careful not to add on more debt.)

The trick is to live on the 70 percent in the middle. In some cases of great financial chaos, it will take time to bring correction. But the 10-70-20 formula can be applied immediately to begin the process.

GREED

Nothing will push us into the quicksand of debt more than greed. Greed is best defined as mishandled blessings.

Wanting to Hold On

A couple in the early days of the church fell prey to greed and reaped a disaster. You'll find their story in Acts 5.

A man named Ananias, with his wife Sapphira, sold a piece of property, and kept back some of the price for himself, with his wife's full knowledge, and bringing a portion of it, he laid it at the apostles' feet. But Peter said, "Ananias, why has Satan filled your heart to lie to the Holy Spirit and to keep back some of the price of the land? While it remained unsold, did it not remain your own? And after it was sold, was it not under your control? Why is it that you have conceived this deed in your heart? You have not lied to men but to God." And as he heard these words, Ananias fell down and breathed his last; and great fear came upon all who heard of it. The young men got up and covered him up, and after carrying him out, they buried him.

Now there elapsed an interval of about three hours, and his wife came in, not knowing what had happened. And Peter responded to her, "Tell me whether you sold the land for such and such a price?" And she said, "Yes, that was the price." Then Peter said to her, "Why is it that you have agreed together to put the Spirit of the Lord to the test? Behold, the feet of those who have buried your husband are at the door, and they will carry you out as well." And immediately she fell at his feet and breathed her last, and the young men came in and found her dead, and they carried her out and buried her beside her husband. (Acts 5:1–10)

God had blessed Ananias and Sapphira with a good profit from the sale of their land, but they weren't *willing* to give to the full extent of their ability because of their greed. They wanted to hold on to as much for themselves as possible, yet give the false impression that they were as generous as possible.

Greed causes many modern husbands and wives to think they *can't* give to the extent they should. That mind-set pushes them deeper and deeper into the quicksand of debt, which then becomes a "reason" for not giving.

"What Would You Do for $10 Million?"

James Patterson and Peter Kim have measured the attitudes of Americans on a number of topics, including greed. They asked people across the country: "What would you be willing to do for $10 million?" Many respondents said they would do at least one—and some, several—of the following:

- abandon their family (25 percent)
- abandon their church (25 percent)
- become prostitutes for a week (23 percent)

- give up their United States citizenship (16 percent)
- leave their spouse (16 percent)
- withhold testimony so a murderer could go free (10 percent)
- kill a stranger (7 percent)
- put up their children for adoption (3 percent)[4]

HOW TO OVERCOME GREED

My oldest son, Ed, pastors the Fellowship Church in Grapevine, Texas. In one series of messages, which he later published as a book, he described four ways to overcome greed:[5]

1. Learn the secret of admiring without desiring.

When you see something attractive in a store window, learn to say, "Wow, that's awesome!" rather than, "Wow, that's awesome—and I must have it!" Couples who develop this ability avoid the quicksand of debt by beating greed.

2. Learn the secret of giving stuff away.

Every three months Ed gives away something he values. What a great practice to adopt! "It helps me stay free of greed and to put things into perspective," Ed says.

As a freshman at the University of Alabama, I worked my way through school. I also attended the First Baptist Church of Tuscaloosa, which had a building program underway. The leadership solicited pledges for the project by visiting every member of the church. After considering the request, I felt I should make a pledge so large for my meager income that the pledge would be unaffordable. The only way I could pay it would be to trust God for the amount I pledged.

Later that year, God called me into full-time ministry. I knew I would transfer from the University of Alabama and go to another school, so I began packing—and saw that pledge card. I had paid one year on my pledge and had two years to go. I looked at my checkbook and saw I had a bit more than I needed to finish paying the pledge.

I began to think about how I was leaving and would no longer be a member of First Baptist, Tuscaloosa. I would be somewhere else in two years! But I couldn't get rid of that pledge card. I couldn't throw it away and I couldn't hide it. So before I left, I wrote a check for those last two years of the pledge. It took just about every penny I had.

The moment I did that, I crucified the greed that tempted me with the possibility of not honoring my commitment.

3. Learn the secret of being generous toward God.

While mishandling of finances doomed Ananias and Sapphira, another greedy man, Zacchaeus, found rescue from that trap. Jesus so impacted this wheeler-dealer that he immediately pledged half his possessions to the poor and restitution to everyone he had defrauded. And Jesus responded to his commitment by saying, "Today salvation has come to this house" (Luke 19:9).

Giving did not save Zacchaeus. Yet it did provide a sign that he had made an about-face from his greed and had become a new man in Christ. He had begun to move toward the generosity that God desires for all His children.

4. Learn the reality of death in relationship to things.

I love the way Ed puts it: "Death marks the final failure of things. We might flash our cash on this earth, but we cannot take anything with us when we die."

Once I received a letter from a man who understood the importance of death with respect to his possessions. He wrote:

> I was a member of a group that consisted of a thousand members, each pledging a million dollars to [fulfilling] the

great commission [of Christ]. After a few years of retirement and living the good life, I returned to the oil and gas business and real estate investments. My wife and I have always given a minimum of the tithe for a few years, and ultimately gave 50 percent of our gross income. However, things did not go well.

As you know, both the oil and gas business and real estate suffered greatly in the middle and late 1980s. I lost most of what I thought would be a lifetime retirement. You told the story about J. P. Getty's experience of looking through a plain window and seeing people, but when he looked at a mirror, he saw only himself. The lesson was that when a little silver is added to the glass we look through, we see only ourselves. This is exactly what happened to me.

I was looking primarily at me and was impressed with what I had done. Even though I was faithful in giving, my motive was spoiled by my pride in doing so. The Lord had to straighten me out. I don't have any idea what He has in store for my future here on this earth, but I know I will spend eternity in heaven. I have asked for His forgiveness. I now have Social Security and my part-time income from which to tithe, and my wife and I do so with great joy and thanksgiving. It is much more rewarding tithing from little, than when I gave 50 percent from a lot.

As this man's wealth died through an economic downturn, his heart died to his wealth. He began to focus on eternity and realized that none of his earthly possessions would track him there—except those he had invested in eternal things.

THE BANDIT OF DECEIT

Another push into the quicksand of debt comes from deceit. Before they tried to deceive anyone else, Ananias and Sapphira deceived themselves. But they could not deceive God.

I remember a classic Jack Benny sketch. As he walks down the street, a robber pulls a gun on him. "Your money or your life!" the thug demands. Benny doesn't say a word. The stick-up man repeats, "Your money or your life!" Jack Benny answers, "I'm thinking about it, I'm thinking about it!"

Many husbands and wives deceive themselves about material possessions for so long they forget that many things in their marriage are more valuable than gold. So they slosh further out into the quagmire of debt, thinking it a normal lifestyle.

Somewhere along the way, they sputter, "but . . . but . . ." Then it's too late. The quicksand of debt pulls them down and the marriage dies.

THE DANGER OF RATIONALIZING

Foundational to the self-deception of Ananias and Sapphira was their rationalization. Perhaps they figured they deserved to hold on to the full amount. Certainly they rationalized that no one would know the full extent of their profit. Doubtless they fell back on the old excuse that what they had was really no one's business.

Such was the problem with the man we know as the "rich young ruler." He wanted to know how to be Jesus' disciple. The Lord told him to sell everything he had, give it to the poor, pull up his stakes, and follow Him. (By the way, that's not Jesus' requirement for everyone but for those who, like this man, allow their possessions to own them.) Doubtless the young man's mind raced with rationalizations about why he deserved to keep his money and the absurdity of Jesus' requirement.

Jesus, who "knew what was in man" (John 2:25), understood the error in the rich young ruler's life. Through years of rationalizing, a transfer of wealth had taken place—not from the young man to another person, but from one part of the man to another.

When your money leaves your hand and gets into your heart, that's when you're in the greatest danger of sinking into the quicksand of debt.

Another Bible character, Demas, suffered from the same problem. Paul wrote to Timothy, "Make every effort to come to me soon; for Demas, having loved this present world, has deserted me and gone to Thessalonica" (2 Timothy 4:9–10).

Don't fall into the same trap. Too many couples have shown an initial love for Christ and His church; then, when affluence came, they rationalized their way down paths away from God. Make sure you don't wander into the same quicksand.

FAILURE TO EXERCISE STEWARDSHIP

Ananias and Sapphira began by asking how much they could keep for themselves. That mind-set led directly to their demise. They should have started by asking how much they could give for the cause of Christ and His kingdom.

Jesus said we are to seek first God's kingdom, and the things we need will come as a result of such prioritizing. Jesus also says, "Where your treasure is, that's where your heart is" (Matthew 6:21, author's paraphrase).

Show me an individual with a proper understanding of wealth, possessions, and money, and I'll show you an individual who understands the deep things of God. But show me someone who is not faithful with his or her money, who does not have a biblical view of possessions, and I'll show you someone (regardless of the religious jargon on his or her lips) who suffers from a major spiritual problem.

How much money can a person have and still be a Spirit-filled, sincere man or woman of God? Is there a limit?

Without question, there is. The limit is this: *When our spiritual wealth lags behind our physical wealth, we have too much money.* When our commitment to God, His Word, and the church comes in second place behind our commitment to material things, we've gone too far and outdistanced the amount of money we should hang on to.

God does one of two things about this. God may let us choke on money by allowing us to earn so much we drown in its power. Or He may take the money away from us, one way or another, depending on the purpose He has for our lives. It all depends on what happens with the wealth we have accumulated, whether it's a little or a lot. The Bible says if we're faithful in the small things, God will give us a chance to be stewards and faithful over much (Matthew 25:21).

When God gives us more than the basics, He wants to use our abundance as a blessing to others, for His kingdom—for things that will last forever. And the man or woman who does not realize this is a fool, by God's own definition. His words are clear: "God said to him, 'You fool! This very night your soul is required of you; and now who will own what you have prepared?'" (Luke 12:20).

Tragically, Ananias and Sapphira fit that description. They wandered intentionally into the quicksand and it swallowed them up.

But no couple has to step into the quicksand of debt and stay there until the marriage suffocates. God gives all of us the opportunity and the ability to use the money He entrusts to us in a way that glorifies Him and blesses others. You don't have to remain an Ananias or a Sapphira. Starting today, you can choose to become a Zacchaeus and prove by your faithful stewardship that money is not your god. And then the words of Jesus can bless your home as they did that of a former tax collector: "Today salvation has come to this house."[6]

REFLECTING ON YOUR RELATIONSHIP

1. What is the driving force of debt in your family?
2. What purchase are you currently considering that would increase your debt? Why do you need it?
3. What percentage of your income are you giving to the church?
4. How much is your current credit card debt? Noncredit card debt? What steps are you taking to get out of debt?

A PERSONAL WORD
Thou Shalt Flee Sexual Temptation— Online and Otherwise

This chapter needs to be read slowly and prayerfully. Victory in this area of your life will enable you to hear the "sound of the trumpets" every morning. Adultery is the Evil One's nuclear bomb. Run to Jesus Christ—He will set you free!

—E. Y.

Commandment 6

THOU SHALT FLEE SEXUAL TEMPTATION— ONLINE AND OTHERWISE

I don't need to quote statistics to convince you that we live in a time and a culture obsessed with sex. It's all too easy to find ourselves listening to, gawking at, and engaging in activities that corrupt the purpose of sex, which is to promote closeness and intimacy between a husband and wife.

So far, our commandments have been about things we need to do if we want to have happy, healthy marriages. Now we must consider something from which the Bible says we need to *flee,* and that's the basis of my sixth commandment of marriage: *Thou shalt flee sexual temptation—online and otherwise.*

As this commandment suggests, our flight isn't only from the temptation to sin physically but from anything that takes our focus away from the one person with whom God has said we are to share ourselves sexually: our spouse. Too many of us believe that so long as we don't commit physical adultery, we aren't doing anything wrong, hurtful, or damaging.

In a moment we'll look at some of the things that can distract us from our spouses and from God's intentions for sex. But first let's take a look at two famous—and contrasting—biblical examples of how to handle sexual temptation.

NO ONE'S IMMUNE

David, the second king of Israel, shows us that no one is immune to sexual temptation—not even a man after God's own heart (see 1 Samuel 13:14).

> Now, when evening came David arose from his bed and walked around on the roof of the king's house, and from the roof he saw a woman bathing; and the woman was very beautiful in appearance. So David sent and inquired about the woman. And one said, "Is this not Bathsheba, the daughter of Eliam, the wife of Uriah the Hittite?" David sent messengers and took her, and when she came to him, he lay with her; and when she had purified herself from her uncleanness, she returned to her house. The woman conceived; and she sent and told David, and said, "I am pregnant." (2 Samuel 11:2–5)

This passage shows us how sexual temptation works. David got a peek at someone pleasing to the eye and he wanted her. Since he saw no one else around that night—including Bathsheba's own husband—the king decided he'd get what he wanted. Who would know? Only he and Bathsheba would be the wiser. And besides, who would dare to challenge the king?

David had his way with Bathsheba, then sent her away. But what a mess this moment of pleasure created for David! And it would get worse before it got better. A lot worse.

Bathsheba's pregnancy prompted a tragic chain of decisions by David. He sent for her husband, Uriah—as faithful a servant to the kingdom as any king could desire—and told him to spend the night with his mate. "You've fought hard and you deserve a night with your wife," David told the old soldier. But Uriah refused. He told David he could never go home and eat and drink and sleep with his wife while the rest of Israel's army remained on the battlefield.

So David moved to Plan B. Since Uriah wouldn't go home to his wife, David sent this brave, faithful soldier to the front, plotting with his military brass to get the man killed in battle. Their evil plans worked. When messengers brought word that the enemy had killed Uriah, David married Bathsheba.

But the king's sin did not go unnoticed by God. The Lord sent the prophet Nathan to confront David. Ironically, David's own words condemned him. Nathan told David a story about a rich, powerful man who forcibly took from a poor man all that he had. David felt outraged and told Nathan, "That man should die for what he's done!"

"You are the man!" cried Nathan.

David had not "gotten away with" anything. He tried to hide his sin for almost a year and probably thought he'd pulled it off. But his cleverness fell short; God knew everything he'd done. And it was only a matter of time before He brought correction to His servant, the king.

While God spared David's life, the chastened ruler still had to live with the consequences of his sinful actions. The son Bathsheba bore to David lived just a week before he died, leaving David brokenhearted. He grieved not just for the loss of his son, but for the heartbreak of having dishonored his God.

After David repented, God once more blessed the king. He even used David's relationship with Bathsheba to further His own kingdom. But He did so only *after* David had suffered greatly for what he had done.[1]

ON YOUR MARK, GET SET . . .

The story of Joseph is shorter and not nearly so complicated as David's, simply because he did what he should have done when temptation presented itself (or should I say, "herself"?). He didn't stand in place and try to deal with it; he just ran.[2]

A powerful man named Potiphar served on Pharaoh's personal staff, and Joseph served Potiphar. In Joseph, Potiphar saw a young man of great integrity. He also noticed that Joseph enjoyed great success in everything he did. Therefore, Potiphar put Joseph in charge of his household and all his business dealings.

Joseph impressed many observers in addition to Potiphar. The Bible tells us the handsome Joseph caught the eye of Potiphar's wife. She knew at first glance that she wanted him, and she was used to getting what she wanted. So day after day she persisted in pressuring Joseph to sleep with her.

It was no small feat for Joseph to run from Mrs. Potiphar's advances. But he told her, "Your husband, my master, trusts me with everything in this household—*including you!* There's no way I can betray him or dishonor God by doing something like this. So forget it!"

But Potiphar's wife had no intention of taking "no" for an answer. Oh, she gave up trying to persuade Joseph with words. But one day, with no one else around, she grabbed Joseph by the shirt and demanded that he sleep with her. As a strong young man, Joseph easily could have overpowered her and perhaps have made her see things his way. But instead of trying to use force or logic, he ran from her. He got away so fast he literally ran out of his shirt, leaving it in the hands of Potiphar's wife (Genesis 39:12–13).

And how did Potiphar's wife respond to this humiliation? She falsely accused Joseph of attempted rape. The authorities threw the young man in prison, but Joseph, still a faithful servant of God, enjoyed the Lord's blessing even behind bars. In no time at all he was running the facility as the warden's "right-hand man." And many months later he rose to second in command over all Egypt, answering only to Pharaoh himself. His powerful position allowed him to save Israel from famine and certain destruction.

Joseph's story demonstrates what great blessings can come when we faithfully follow God's commands. It also sets a great example of how to handle persistent sexual temptation that threatens to overwhelm us: *run!*

RUN—DON'T WALK—FROM TEMPTATION

The Old Testament has no monopoly on the theme of fleeing sexual temptation. In his first letter to the Corinthians, Paul calls our bodies temples of the Holy Spirit. Every other sin, he says, we commit against God, but sexual immorality is a sin against both God *and our own bodies.* The residents of Corinth knew a good bit about sexual immorality; many *flocked to* it rather than *fled from* it. But Paul instructed them to flee (1 Corinthians 6:18).

The apostle repeated this command to a young pastor named Timothy. Like most young men, Timothy apparently struggled with lust. So Paul instructed his young friend to "flee also youthful lusts" (2 Timothy 2:22 KJV). This remains a word not just to husbands and wives but to those who are yet to be married. The Bible teaches that our bodies are gifts reserved for our future mates. What a wonderful wedding gift to bring to your own marriage!

The Bible, both Old and New Testaments, never encourages us to try to avoid struggling with sexual temptation. It insists that we get out of its path altogether!

TREAT SEXUAL TEMPTATION
LIKE A DEADLY DISEASE

Suppose you heard that a deadly disease had broken out in a remote area. Only trained medical professionals dared to travel to the outbreak site, and you knew that if you contracted this disease, most likely you would die. You also knew that only those who traveled to the location of the epidemic could be exposed to the disease.

Would it be brave or just plain stupid to travel to the affected area, just to prove how "resistant" you were to the deadly bacteria? No right-minded person would put himself or herself into such danger without good reason. Yet that is exactly what many Christians do regarding sexual temptation. Before and during marriage they dabble in it, flirt with it, and entertain it—believing that at the last minute they will be able to slam on the brakes and keep from crashing.

It doesn't work that way. God knows us. He "wired" us, so He knows how sexual temptation can exert a powerful tug on His children. That's why He instructs us to flee. If we treated sexual temptation like a highly contagious, deadly disease, we would better understand and obey the Bible's admonition to flee.

DESIGNER SEX

It's God's Plan

A few years ago, I wrote a book entitled *Pure Sex.* In one of its chapters I outlined four things I believe everyone should know about sex. First, *sex is God's idea.* Humans did not invent or improve on sex, no matter what Dr. Ruth, Hugh Hefner, Madonna, or others might suggest. God created sex; better yet, He designed it, and not merely for procreation. God designed sex to be an act of joyful pleasure by which a husband and wife bond physically, spiritually, and emotionally—they become one.

Second, *human sexuality is unique.* Society would have us to believe that we are simply part of the animal kingdom, nothing more. "It's only natural," goes the cultural mantra. But sex is designed not as a mere consequence of instinct but as an enjoyable, intimate bond between a husband and wife, both for procreation and pleasure. Though the world might have us believe that we've evolved to a level just above the *animals,* God tells us we were created just slightly below the *angels.* The Bible says we are created in the image of God. In fact, humans are the "crown" of creation (see Psalm 8:5). Human sexuality, therefore, is unique.

Third, *sex involves every aspect of our being.* In God's divine plan, He made Eve to "complete" Adam. She really was his "better half" and filled the void in his life that none of the animals could. She was bone of his bones and flesh of his flesh—in other words, just what he needed! Once Adam realized this, God created marriage. "Therefore shall a man leave his father and his mother, and shall cleave unto his wife: and they shall be one flesh" (Genesis 2:24 KJV). Sex involves total oneness with our mates, just as it did with that first couple: physically, yes, but also psychologically, emotionally, and spiritually.

That's one reason sex before marriage is unhealthy—it brings people together in an intimacy designed exclusively for marriage. It creates bonds that are intended for marriage alone. That's why *sex requires boundaries,* our fourth point. God created sex as a sacred act between two people committed to one another in the covenant relationship of marriage. Because of its sacredness, the expression of love and oneness between a husband and wife must be protected and honored. "Marriage is to be held in honor among all, and the marriage bed is to be undefiled" (Hebrews 13:4).

But the sexual union goes even deeper than that.

It's God's Symbol

Intercourse between a husband and wife symbolizes the way God interacts with His people. As an act of incredible love, God seeks intimacy with us. You can hear the lover's heart in the way God addresses Israel through His prophet Ezekiel:

"I passed by you and saw you, and behold, you were at the time for love; so I spread My skirt over you and covered your nakedness. I also swore to you and entered into a covenant with you so that you became Mine," declares the LORD God. "Then I bathed you with water, washed off your blood from you and anointed you with oil. I also clothed you with embroidered cloth and put sandals of porpoise skin on your feet; and I wrapped you with fine linen and covered you with silk. I adorned you with ornaments, put bracelets on your hands and a necklace around your neck. I also put a ring in your nostril, earrings in your ears and a beautiful crown on your head. Thus you were adorned with gold and silver, and your dress was of fine linen, silk and embroidered cloth. You ate fine flour, honey and oil; so you were exceedingly beautiful and advanced to royalty." (Ezekiel 16:8–13)

God treated His covenant with Israel as a marriage. Some interpreters see the Old Testament's Song of Solomon not only as a poetic statement of Solomon's love for his wife, but also of God for His people. The New Testament depicts the church as the bride of Christ.

So, sex between a husband and wife has the additional sanctity of symbolizing God's great, intimate love toward His created beings. Therefore, sex outside of marriage is the equivalent of idolatry.

How do we protect the sacredness of marriage? We heed Scripture and flee sexual temptation. How? By running from it like a deadly disease, by recognizing the "purity" of sex as God designed it, and by protecting it from the onslaughts of a society that has degraded sex to a passionate "pastime."

CULTURAL SEX

Although God gave sex to married couples as His sacred gift, our culture has cheapened that gift. For many, sex has become nothing more than a recreational activity, a fun diversion unrelated to any kind of love or commitment.

Most people who have been married a long time would agree that it's more difficult to maintain a healthy marriage today than two decades ago. The cultural environment exerts tremendous pressure on husbands and wives.

As America and the world raced toward a new millennium, pollster George Gallup surveyed trends that were impacting marriage and that would continue to have an effect in the twenty-first century. The research clearly showed pressures building against homes and families.

Alternative Lifestyles

The first cultural trend threatening marriage is an increase in "alternative lifestyles." From 1960 to 1997, the American marriage rate decreased by 33 percent.[3] A key reason is people are living together increasingly in arrangements other than the traditional husband-wife relationship. Gallup found there was a tenfold increase in men and women living together in a sexual arrangement from 1960 to 1998, with a 50 percent rise in the 1990s.

Gallup reported only a sixth of such relationships lasted three years and a mere tenth endured for a decade. He also discovered the probability of cohabiting couples marrying has declined, while the chances of a breakup of such relationships prior to marriage has increased by 20 percent.[4]

Alternative lifestyles include same-sex cohabitation and unions. Hawaii and Vermont are just two American states among several where there is pressure for same-sex marriages. Gallup and other research organizations find the views of many Americans moderating regarding the acceptance of homosexuality, and so the trend is likely to increase.

Sexual Immorality

Gallup says the second threat to marriage and family is sexual immorality. Try to think of a time in the last five years when a television drama or motion picture has shown husband and wife in a physical relationship. Chances are that the couple you see sleeping together on the big and small screens are *not* husband and wife.

Infidelity in marriage leads to divorce, and a fractured home often harms children. In the worst cases, children without fathers in their home rebel against society. The statistics are shocking:

- 72 percent of the nation's teen murderers come from fatherless homes.
- 70 percent of long-term prison inmates grew up in homes without dads.
- 60 percent of people who commit rape were raised in homes where the father was absent.[5]

Clearly, America needs to return to the basics when it comes to sex. God created this beautiful relationship. Why? Obviously for procreation, pleasure, *and our protection.*

We need to flee sexual temptation and immorality and return to "pure sex." How can we do this?

STAY OFF THE ROOFTOP!

Do you really want to flee sexual temptation? Then "stay off the rooftop."

David got himself into big trouble, first of all, by being at the wrong place at the wrong time. While Israel faced down its enemies on the battlefield, King David chose to stay home. Instead of leading his nation into war, he fell into the hands of an enemy more powerful than an opposing army.

Next, he dwelt on his physical attraction to another man's wife. He reveled in the eye candy provided by Bathsheba's rooftop bathing that night, but that is not what got him into trouble. David set himself up for a fall when he allowed himself to prolong his lustful stares. As he stared at Bathsheba's beauty, his heart fell prey to lust and desire.

Those Rooftops at Work, in the Neighborhood, and at "Clubs"

Today, many of us—men and women alike—face our own rooftops. We don't have to wander outside to see our "Bathshebas." Our work environment or neighborhood might provide a rooftop. I know of many men and women, including those who work in full-time ministry, who've struggled with lustful thoughts toward an attractive or charming coworker. Others have endured that same struggle with a neighbor, family friend, or associate.

Men need only drive to the nearest town with a so-called "men's club" featuring female bodies on display. There is also an increasing number of clubs for women where male dancers leave little to the imagination.

The Online Rooftop

But perhaps our closest equivalent to David's staring at Bathsheba would be peering into the cold blue of a computer screen filled with pornography. Far too many people spend evenings as David did that fateful night—gazing, contemplating, and fantasizing over what they're viewing.

With the arrival of the Internet, we don't even have to leave the friendly confines of home to get on a "rooftop." A man who works in the computer industry recently told me that in just one year Americans shelled out $1.4 billion for content off the Internet. Of that $1.4 billion, more than 70 percent went to pay for "adult" content. That's nearly a billion dollars a year just for X-rated material. And all of it waits in the comfort of your own office or den chair, readily available for viewing!

It doesn't take an Einstein to see how this can devastate the sexual intimacy and trust between a husband and wife. I can't begin to tell you how many marriages I've seen damaged, or even ruined, by the effects of pornography. It's so easy to rationalize: *I didn't actually touch another woman. I was just looking.*

Beware that kind of mind-set! Whenever we allow our minds to go somewhere sexually other than where God wants our focus—on our spouses—then it's only a matter of time before our bodies follow. Consider an example from the world of drugs. Some suggest (others insist) that the use of "gateway" drugs, such as marijuana, leads to the use of "harder" chemicals like heroin and cocaine. Just about everyone who uses heroin or cocaine began their drug use with "softer" narcotics.

I believe the same is true regarding sex. A man who views pornography or engages in sex chats may not realize he's creating an insatiable craving for more. And soon, that which is only virtual can become physical. It's only a matter of time before he allows his body to follow where his mind already has traveled.

A Fall from the Online Rooftop

I received a letter from a man I've known for more than fifteen years. At one time this man walked with God. He and his wife both professed Christ and stayed very active in church. But somehow he allowed himself to get dragged into a world of sin and tragedy that started with some "harmless fun" on the Internet.

In a typewritten letter of several pages, he confessed how he had become sexually frustrated in his marriage and started looking for an outlet. As a Christian, he didn't want an adulterous affair. Instead, he tried a "safe" release for his frustrations: the Internet.

This man began viewing all sorts of pornographic material. He also spent time in adult chat rooms where he took part in lewd sexual conversations with total strangers. Not long after he started using the Internet, he "met" a woman from another state with marital problems similar to his. They "chatted" on their computers regularly, exchanged pictures, and eventually talked on the phone. Their conversations seemed free and natural, and soon their chats turned sexual. After a few weeks, they took what seemed the most logical next step: they decided to meet in person. And immediately they began an adulterous affair.

I wish I could say that the man saw how wrong he was, repented, and got to work repairing the damage he'd done to his marriage. But that didn't happen. Convinced he was "in love," he divorced his wife, leaving her alone to care for their children. His paramour did the same, and the two were quickly married.

Jesus once told His disciples that anyone who looks lustfully on a woman has already committed adultery in his heart (Matthew 5:28). His statement should warn us to guard our eyes, our minds, and our hearts from things that would cause us to lust. But it also suggests that our Lord knew something about how the mind and the heart eventually lead the body to engage in destructive activities.

Therefore, with your mind, with your eyes, with your heart, and with your body—*flee* from sexual temptation.

FLEE TO WHAT?

I love the way God always gives us a "to." In order to avoid the dangerous pitfall of sexual temptation and build happy, successful marriages, we need to flee *to* deep, genuine, and biblical intimacy with our mates.

Sexual intimacy takes time. That's a key lesson of the greatest sex manual ever written: the Bible, and it's highlighted in Song of Solomon, a little book the Holy Spirit tucked away in the Old Testament. Many godly men and women throughout history have struggled with this short book; some scholars in the Middle Ages even wondered if it should be included in the Bible.

Some contend that the Song of Solomon is only an allegorical look at God's love for His people, of Christ's love for His bride, the church. While I believe the allegory is there, I also take this book at face value. It's a fabulous work that uses vivid, sensual language to describe God's ideal of romantic, intimate love between husband and wife.

The Song of Solomon provides black-and-white proof that God both designed and created sex and sexual intimacy within marriage. It gives a memorable account of the passionate love between Solomon and his wife, the Shulammite. The Song of Solomon gives us a beautiful picture of growing, maturing love and intimacy. And in it we discover practical principles for building sexual intimacy.

IT'S ABOUT TIME

Intimacy Takes Time

Sexual intimacy takes time. In the first chapter of his book, Solomon gives us a snapshot of the love between him and the Shulammite when they're engaged. Notice Solomon talks about her from the head up, because that's all he can see. They're not yet married, so the rest of her remains covered.

By chapter 4, Solomon and the Shulammite have been married for a while and the description becomes more intimate and detailed. Solomon writes of his wife's eyes, her hair, and her breasts—things a man in love appreciates in his mate.

By the time we reach chapter 7, Solomon and the Shulammite have written some history together, like all married couples. They've weathered crises, pain, and problems, yet their love survives and thrives. Now Solomon praises his wife from the top of her head to the bottom of her feet. They've spent much time together and have grown in intimacy. Only through time can a couple achieve closeness like this.

Intimacy Takes Good Timing

One morning Solomon made advances toward the Shulammite. Her response: "Not this morning, honey. It's too early." Apparently Solomon forgot to check his sundial. He stalks away.

An hour or so later, his wife is fully awake and now desires to be with Solomon, so she goes looking for him. But the sexual clocks of this husband and wife were not synchronized on this particular day and they lost a golden opportunity for sexual intimacy.

If in real estate the issue is location, location, location, then in sex, it's timing, timing, timing! And that means timely communication.

The Song of Solomon is about discourse as much as it is about intercourse. To develop deep, lasting, passionate intimacy in your marriage, you must communicate. Study the interchanges between Solomon and his wife. They speak to one another in amorous terms and use intimate code words reserved for their romance.

Only in recent times has "intercourse" been narrowed down to mean just a sexual act. In earlier periods the word referred to various means of interaction between individuals. The verbal intercourse between Solomon and the Shulammite is as exciting and vibrant as their embrace in bed. In fact, their romantic verbal interchange enhances their enjoyment of physical sex.

The Song of Solomon shows that God intends for sex between

a husband and wife to be exciting and pleasurable. Couples would do well to read it together.

Intimacy Takes Time Away Together

Someone has said that one of the surest ways to bring an end to marital intimacy is to have children. While having a family makes maintaining marital intimacy a challenge, it doesn't have to spell an end to intimacy.

Children are a wonderful blessing from the Lord, but they also demand a lot of time. Most Christian couples work for a living and also tend to other life responsibilities, including those at church and with friends and extended family. That can lead to a pretty demanding schedule, and when parental responsibilities mount, it can seem overwhelming. Finding intimacy in such a setting isn't easy, but I can tell you from experience that it can be done!

One key is for couples to make time for one another, to plan to spend time away from the hustle and bustle of everyday family life. Solomon knew the importance of getting away:

> Come, my beloved, let us go out into the country,
> Let us spend the night in the villages.
> Let us rise early and go to the vineyards;
> Let us see whether the vine has budded
> And its blossoms have opened,
> And whether the pomegranates have bloomed.
> There I will give you my love. (Song of Solomon 7:11–12)

Solomon and the Shulammite understood what so many couples today have forgotten: Sometimes you just need to get away and spend time together with no distractions. Take the time to "go out into the country," to "spend the night in the village," and to focus your attention on one another. This allows true marital intimacy to continue growing.

BUILDING MARITAL INTIMACY ON THE ROCK

Our world is filled with all kinds of marital pitfalls and land mines. Yet some marriages don't merely survive in this world of temptations but actually thrive in it. How do they do it?

Jesus answers the question in His parable of the two foundations. The Lord gave us a picture of two houses: one founded upon a rock, which stood up against the storm, and another built upon sand, which soon collapsed. The same storm had blown against both houses with the same intensity of wind, torrential rain, and flooding (see Matthew 7:24–27). The wild gale tore at the structures, the rain pounded the surface of the ground, and the floodwaters seeped into the foundations. Every point of the buildings was attacked.

The same is true of our marriages. Sexual temptation attacks every point of the marriage structure, all the way down to its foundation. How can we build to survive the storm?

Paul writes that "like a wise master builder I laid a foundation, and another is building on it. But each man must be careful how he builds on it. For no man can lay a foundation other than the one which is laid, which is Jesus Christ" (1 Corinthians 3:10–11).

When we build our marriages upon the rock of Jesus Christ and His principles, they will withstand every kind of wind that blows—even the fierce gale of sexual temptation.

You may wonder, *What about my marriage? It's on shaky ground and it's being pounded by the storm! What do I do?* Let me encourage you with some practical, insightful, and *comforting* advice.

WHEN THE GOING GETS TOUGH . . .

We've heard it quoted in numerous situations: "When the going gets tough, the tough get going." Some well-meaning soul has usually shared these words with us in a low moment —when we're down-and-out, about to give up. Because of its familiarity, we may have missed the profound truth behind this statement.

Just as a coach would encourage his team to toughen up and get back to the fundamentals to overcome defeat, God would have us review some of the basics He's provided for us. The Bible is filled with truths and promises from God. Certain ones are stated outright; others are understood from the content and context of a passage or principle.

Three of these truths can help us through the toughest of life's challenges—even the strongest temptations and deepest hurts. They are: (1) God has a *plan* for our lives; (2) God is *present* in our lives; and (3) God's *protection* guards our lives. Nowhere are these three promises better seen working together than in one of my favorite Old Testament passages, Isaiah 43:1–3. In fact, I would recommend printing Isaiah 43:1–3 on a poster and hanging it on any wall—the locker room, the boardroom, or even the bedroom.

God's Plan

Through the prophet Isaiah, God tells His people, "Do not fear, for I have redeemed you; I have called you by name; you are Mine!" (v. 1). What a tremendous word! God says, "Fear not." Why? Because He has redeemed us through Jesus Christ. And those who know Christ are in God's plan. He knows our names—in fact, He knows our birthdays, our addresses, our Social Security numbers, our phone numbers, even the unlisted ones. God knows the very number of hairs on our heads! So relax. Do not be afraid. God has a plan for your life and your marriage.

He will incorporate the stormy seasons of your marriage into His plan as well as the seasons of "sizzle" between you and your mate. The bad times come when men and women, acting in freedom, make wrong choices. God does not cause the rupturing of relationships, but He will use the experiences of your life for your good and His glory (see Romans 8:28–29).

For example, through the tragic events of September 11, 2001, we learned the revealing story of Todd and Lisa Beamer. This young couple has impacted America with the beauty of their Christian witness, one through his death and the other through her life. As his hijacked jet sped toward our nation's capital, Todd Beamer inspired his fellow passengers and, later, all of us with his final words, "Let's roll!" Todd died that day as he and other heroic passengers managed to divert the hijackers' attack on Washington, D.C., by causing United Airlines Flight 93 to crash into an unpopulated area outside Shanksville, Pennsylvania.

Since that tragic day, his widow, Lisa Beamer, has inspired Americans with her faith and hope. Lisa knows God has a plan for each of His children that neither death nor life can thwart. She trusted God as He led their marriage. Less than one year after her husband's death, she said, "My faith shows me at least a little of God's perspective on our world and on my life, and that there is a good purpose to it all."[6] Lisa used the words of a nineteenth-century pastor and writer, Henry Van Dyke, to express her own confidence in God's plan:

> In some realms of nature, shadows or darkness are the places of greatest growth. The beautiful Indian corn never grows more rapidly than in the darkness. The sun withers and curls the leaves, but once a cloud hides the sun, they quickly unfold. The shadows provide a service that the sunlight cannot.

When your marriage bottoms out because of temptation and its aftermath, it is time to rest in your Father, who says, "Fear not." It's time to trust that in the darkness, He is doing something great according to the plan He ordained for your life.

God's Presence

God has declared through Isaiah, "When you pass through the waters, I will be with you" (43:2). Many married people have been like Simon Peter walking on the water. Do you remember the story? (See Matthew 14:22–33.) Jesus walked on the Sea of Galilee to join His disciples in their boat. In his enthusiasm, Peter asked if he, too, could walk on the water. Jesus said, "Come out to Me." Peter jumped out of the boat onto the water. He did great for a while, until he took his eyes off Jesus and focused on the wind and waves surrounding him. Many a bride and groom have jumped out of the security of their parental home and, like Peter, have walked upon the turbulence around them—until the rolling troubles captured their attention and they began to sink into hopelessness, despair, separation. Some have even sunk into divorce.

The rescue for those whose marriages are sinking is the same as it was for Simon Peter. He reached out and cried "Lord, save me!" Jesus, who was standing nearby, grabbed Peter and lifted him up.

If your marriage is being sucked into the depths because of temptation, trouble, and turmoil, Jesus is as near to you as He was to Simon Peter that night on the Sea of Galilee.

God's Protection

God promises His protection in all seasons, whether you are on top of the waters or sinking. He continues with His promise in Isaiah 43 that when you go "through the rivers, they will not overflow you. [Even] when you walk through the fire, you will not be scorched, nor will the flame burn you" (v. 2).

Notice that God did not say "when you go *around* the river ... the flood ... the fire." He said when you pass *through* those perilous places and conditions. None of us knows what one will have to face, but there is a grim certainty that some of us will pass through raging rivers, torrential floods, and blistering fires. God is frank and honest about the prospects of pain, but He is equally candid about the promise of protection in the midst of those sufferings.

It's troubling also that God says the passage through fire will not be a quick run but a *walk*. A run might be only a matter of moments in the heat, but a walk could mean months, even years.

. . . THE TOUGH GET GOING

For a man named Lewis, the walk was five years in duration. A mysterious disease began a slow, destructive course through his wife's body. At first it appeared she would go quickly, but it was not to be. Day by day, week by week, month by month, year by year—she slowly slipped away from him.

Lewis's days were spent working hard, trying to earn a living. His nights were given to his wife's care. There were no fun-filled weekends. Just more sadness, more pain.

On top of it all, Lewis was a healthy man, still sexually alive. Temptation was all around him. Voices whispered that his wife was, for all practical purposes, dead, and that there would be no sin in entering a sexual relationship with another woman. Lewis battled self-pity: *I hurt so much watching my wife die, why should I have to suffer this burning desire too?* The logic seemed so simple, so right.

Yet Lewis did not yield. Something in his heart kept him faithful to his wife, now comatose. The "something" that caused Lewis to remain faithful was his own *faithfulness to the marriage covenant* he had made with his wife a decade earlier and his *commitment to* God.[7]

It was a long, slow walk through the fire for Lewis. But when his wife died, he stood with honor before her casket, knowing he had kept the covenant of faithfulness, even when people close to him said he was no longer bound.

This is the way we overcome the fires of temptation. We press into God, even when we can no longer draw close to a spouse who has left us or is unfaithful to us. Such intimacy with the Father will enable us to walk so successfully through the fire that there will not even be the smell of smoke upon us!

REFLECTING ON YOUR RELATIONSHIP

1. Write your definition of sex. Would your understanding of sex be more in keeping with "designer" sex or "cultural" sex?
2. What "rooftops" tempt you most? What is your "flight" plan from this temptation?
3. What grade would you give the intimacy (sexual, emotional, and spiritual) in your marriage? What is one thing you and your mate can do to improve your grade?
4. Is your marriage built on the rock or the sand? Explain.

A PERSONAL WORD
Thou Shalt Forgive Thy Mate—
490 Times and More.

Never lay down an ultimatum to your mate.
When two become one—that's marriage—you
are committed to forgiving the "better half" of
yourself for a lifetime. Stop clubbing your mate
with "yesterday"! This chapter will tell you
how to genuinely forgive.

—E. Y.

THOU SHALT FORGIVE THY MATE— 490 TIMES AND MORE

B ob and Mary's marriage brought them nothing but misery. They argued almost continually, their children constantly rebelled, and the house always looked like a pigsty. They held differing ideas on lifestyle, marriage, and rearing children. Over time, their splintered home filled with anger, bitterness, and strife. A major tragedy seemed inevitable.

Bob's work as a sales representative took him out of town two or three nights a week. On one of these trips, he met a young divorcee named Shirley. They got together for a meal "just to talk," and soon an affair developed. When Mary found out, she confronted Bob—and he promptly left home.

It took only a few months for Bob to realize that he didn't love Shirley. In the depths of his heart, despite the problems at home, he knew that he still loved his wife. He desperately wanted to work things out, but he wondered if Mary could forgive him.

Although Bob had committed adultery, both he and Mary

had a lot of forgiving to do. The affair simply capped off years of neglect, unkindness, selfishness, and indifference. Both parties had a lot of ground to cover if they were to save their marriage.

A TOUGH QUESTION

Many couples today face the same thorny question that confronted Bob and Mary: *Can our marriage survive adultery?* The question has a great deal to do with my seventh marriage commandment: *Thou shalt forgive thy mate—490 times and more.*

As I have talked through the years with husbands and wives, I've discovered that nothing is so tough for a marriage partner to forgive as adultery. One act of infidelity can undermine trust and divide couples like no other wrongdoing.

Of course, no one just wakes up one morning and says, "I think I'll have an affair today." What factors contribute to the development of an affair?

Proximity

For many who fall into the trap of adultery, there's someone at work, or at the Little League games, or at the gym. Gradually, the proximity that had been merely nearness in space becomes the proximity of heart and soul. Often, as in the case of "Bob and Mary," that proximity leads to the closest of all, the physical union. Thus, two hurting people end up hurting others.

Problems

Every family has problems, ranging from stressful relationships with sons and daughters to disagreements over how the house should be kept. As a result, the couple's sexual relationship often fades.

Some people go through what can be described only as the

"middle-aged 'crazies.'" A man in such a tormenting condition is trying to prove his *virility,* while the menopausal woman wants to demonstrate her *desirability.*

Other problems include failure—and even success. Individuals who have failed are hurting and look for affirmation and edification. Sometimes they feel too ashamed to turn to their mate, so they look for another who might "understand." And with success, the person may receive recognition and warm smiles from associates of the opposite sex. The attention and compliments can become alluring.

The Playboy Philosophy

The *Playboy* philosophy can be summed up like this: If something feels good, it must be acceptable. We should recognize and enjoy the pleasures of this life.

This is an errant and destructive philosophy, yet it has become a cultural standard. Some even attempt to paint this distorted perspective with the whitewash of "spirituality." They say that since any biological urge we have must have come from God, it is only right to satisfy it—indeed, it is almost our sacred duty.

Such a propagandized culture regards sexual renegades as heroes. And should the "common folks" not operate at the glamorized level of sexual conquest, they may well feel their own identity under attack.

RESPONDING TO ANY WRONGS

Of course, there are other wrongs that can cause estrangement. Even if the partners stay "faithful" to one another sexually, they continue to hurt one another with acts of insensitivity and unkindness, moments of selfishness, and cruel words. Unless things change, the downward spiral of bitterness will continue.

We can respond in many ineffective (and sometimes

harmful) ways. Some spouses who have been wronged simply *retaliate* and take an "eye for an eye" approach. "I'm going to get you back!" they declare. So the wife says, "You left me with the kids three nights this week. I'm tired of you going out with the guys and then saying you needed a break. So I'm going out to visit *my* friends. Monday I'll be with Sue, Wednesday with Sally, and Friday I'll be visiting Mom."

Others respond with *rebellion*. "OK, George, don't expect me to clean up and get the kids ready for bed next week. You can do it yourself." If the offense is adultery, the spouse says, "I'm outta here! I'm calling a lawyer. We're finished." The one who wants "out" might even justify the decision to leave by recalling that the Bible lists adultery as grounds for divorce. There might even be a call made or a visit taken to a pastor or counselor, so that when the divorce takes place, the "victim" can feel justified that every effort had been made to save the marriage.

Still others respond with *accommodation. Well, I guess that's how men are,* the wife tells herself. *I'll just get the kids ready for bed and do some reading.* But each evening she feels neglected, and the resentment grows. Bitterness is developing, and the marriage is becoming tense. And her husband may not even know why.

For adultery, accommodation is the saddest reaction. The offended spouse simply accepts his or her mate's behavior. So husband and wife exist in a "You do your thing, and I'll do mine" sort of existence. "Let's keep the bills paid, the children fed and clothed, and the appearances good."

These three responses cause as much destruction as the wrong itself. But there is one right response—the response God truly blesses.

He calls it *forgiveness*.

TAKING THE ROUTE OF FORGIVENESS

How can we best deal with the imperfections, flaws, and sins that take place within our marriages? The operative word has to be "forgiveness." We all need to cultivate a lifestyle of forgiveness, a mind-set that forgives consistently and unconditionally.

The Old Testament provides a moving example of unconditional forgiveness and acceptance on the part of a husband. His name was Hosea; his wife was Gomer. In this case the marital transgression was severe—adultery. And the degree of forgiveness would seem to be great. How was Hosea able to forgive his wife?

God had instructed Hosea to marry her, even though Gomer was a wayward woman (Hosea 1:1–3). Apparently the early stage of her marriage to Hosea abounded with mutual love, commitment, and joy. Gomer bore Hosea three children, but before long she had one adulterous affair, then another and another.

Eventually, Gomer left Hosea. She sold herself as a prostitute and soon wound up a slave. When her master put her up for sale, no one made a bid—except one man. In an act of forgiveness, grace, and unconditional, undying love, Hosea bought Gomer and took her home, not as a slave but to be his wife once more (3:1–2). He heard God's word to restore his wife and obeyed God (though notice in v. 3 he called his wife to be faithful once more).

This story of Hosea and Gomer recounts one man's unconditional love and forgiveness for his wife and provides us with a compelling picture of God's love for His wayward, spiritually adulterous people. It's the story of a love that refuses to let go.

The kind of forgiveness that Hosea extended to his wife, God wants us to extend to one another, especially to our mates. Centuries after Hosea's time, Jesus expounded the theme of forgiveness. When Peter asked Jesus, "How often shall my brother sin against me and I forgive him? Up to seven times?" Jesus responded, "I do not say to you, up to seven times, but up to seventy times seven" (Matthew 18:21–22).

I believe ol' Simon Peter would have made a good Texan, at least according to popular stereotypes. He could be brash, boastful, bold, and occasionally belligerent. On this occasion, Peter wanted to show the Lord how well he understood the idea of forgiveness. "If someone offends me and I forgive him seven times for the same offense," he boasted to the Lord, "isn't that enough?"

The rabbis of that day required fellow Jews to forgive an offense three times. Long before anyone thought to invent baseball, these religious leaders had created a "three strikes, you're out" scenario. Once you had forgiven someone three times for the same offense, however, your duty to forgive had expired.

Peter might as well have been saying to Jesus, "Lord, seven times is twice the legal requirement, plus one. Shouldn't that be enough?"

No doubt the burly fisherman expected Jesus to say, "Peter, what a great and gracious man you are! You have learned the message of the kingdom of God better than anybody!" But that's not how Jesus answered.

"No, Peter," the Lord said, "you don't forgive a mere seven times. You forgive seventy *times* seven."

That's 490 times!

The wisdom of Jesus staggers us with its depth. He meant to tell Peter—and all of us—that forgiveness is not merely a onetime, two-time, or even seven-time decision but a way of life. Here's what happens: If you forgive someone 490 times, somewhere around number 300 you get in the *habit* of forgiveness. Forgiveness is to be habitual, a practice that becomes second nature.

And without question, it must become part of a healthy, growing marriage.

SWEAT THE SMALL STUFF

Just about now, you may be thinking that forgiveness is all about the big problems (like adultery). You therefore may have concluded that this chapter doesn't apply to you. You might have decided that you don't need to cultivate the skill of forgiveness, since the major offenses just don't occur in your marriage. Perhaps your mate doesn't "fool around," doesn't drink, doesn't curse, or doesn't physically abuse the family.

Those Little Foxes

It's easy in such a relationship to allow tiny things that don't appear on the marital sonar to lurk below the surface until they show up as huge blips on the screen—all because we don't think such minute offenses need to be forgiven.

King Solomon's wife understood the threats of the "minor" issues. She penned a love sonnet to her husband in which she described him as a sleek creature in pursuit of his mate. Hear her longing cry: "O my dove, in the clefts of the rock, in the secret place of the steep pathway, let me see your form, let me hear your voice; for your voice is sweet, and your form is lovely" (Song of Solomon 2:14).

Then came a strange plea: "Catch the foxes for us, the little foxes that are ruining the vineyards, while our vineyards are in blossom" (v. 15).

Solomon's wife used the harvest as a metaphor for the love relationship the two of them shared. She seemed not at all concerned about the wind or rain or other "big" threats that might destroy the harvest. Rather, she focused on the "little foxes" that squirm through the broken fence and spoil the vines, little by little.

Every marriage has to beware of the little foxes.

Certainly we need to stay away from the "big stuff" that can destroy our relationships. But more than that, we need to offer regular forgiveness for the small stuff, those irritating habits and ways that can drive a wedge between a couple. These "little foxes" bite and rip until they spoil the marriage.

It's been said that marriage is no big thing but a lot of little things. I couldn't agree more. I think of a woman who once told me how her first husband drove her crazy by splattering toothpaste on the bathroom mirror. "I fussed at him constantly," she said. "I never let him alone about it." This "little thing" caused untold conflict and strife in the marriage. The wife simply wouldn't forgive her husband for making a mess when he brushed his teeth.

When Little Things Become Big Threats

Adultery may cause a spouse to swiftly give up on a marriage, but the little things can accumulate and present just as deadly a threat. They root around until two people say, "Our marriage is dead; there is no life left in it."

A couple used those very words to describe the state of their relationship to a marriage counselor. In all the complaining and accusations, however, the counselor noticed that the wife kept referring to her husband as "Hon."

Finally, the counselor looked at her and said, "You say you have no feelings for him, but you keep calling him 'Hon.'"

"Oh yes," she replied, "I've called him that for years. You know, 'Hun,' as in *'Attila the Hun'!*"

Can a woman forgive a man who acts with such brutality that she compares him to one of the world's most noted tyrants? Can a couple find any hope once adultery has punched a tank-sized hole in its protective fence? Can the passion be restored in a marriage devoured by the "little foxes" of constant nagging, bickering, small deceits, and acts of insensitivity?

The answer is yes—*if* the "ground" of the marriage gets covered with forgiveness.

LEVELS OF FORGIVENESS

I believe our marriage vows need to be reworded. Millions of couples have promised "to love, honor, and obey," but perhaps what we really need are commitments to love, honor, obey, and *forgive*.

A marriage is not so much the union of two great lovers as it is of two great forgivers. Great marriages are made up of two people who have committed themselves to daily forgiving one another. That means that Jo Beth and I must recognize, deal with, and forgive the little foxes that steal into our relationship, as well as remain on guard for the big carnivores that lurk on the murky horizon.

Now, just as different levels of offenses exist, so there are different levels of forgiveness. A small offense such as splattering toothpaste or leaving the toilet seat up doesn't require the same kind of forgiveness as an adulterous affair. The former offense may require a partner to forgive daily and to refuse to make a mountain out of a molehill. The latter most certainly may require a great deal of time, prayer, and effort to forgive. These two offenses, vastly different in severity, need different levels of brokenness and repentance. In other words, they require different levels of forgiveness.

Some people think that all they have to do in order to forgive their spouse is to say, "I forgive you," and then never bring up the offense again. But this is not true forgiveness. True forgiveness involves transformation brought about by a deep heart decision. It's not just a change of mind but a change of heart in which the offense gets removed from the record.

Forgiveness doesn't mean tossing a few kind words at the offending partner. Such words get included along the way, but other important issues must come into play for genuine biblical forgiveness to occur.

ISSUES OF THE HEART

Acceptance

We must learn to accept our spouse if we are to deal with an offense. Acceptance simply means acknowledging that the hurtful event actually happened. There is no "undoing" it, not even in this age of revisionist history. We can't change what happened or cover it up for long. Oh, we can offer our excuses or alibis, but the fact remains that the wrong occurred and we have to face the consequences. We have to deal with reality.

Some people tragically deny either that they have been hurt or that they have hurt others. "It's no big deal. I'll just pretend like it never happened and move on—it's just too painful to deal with." But the offense *did* happen. It is an event just as real as Neil Armstrong walking on the moon.

When people fall into denial, a dangerous process ensues. Illusion follows, and such individuals wind up living in a fantasy world. If they spend long enough in that unreal world, they can become totally separated from reality.

It is vital to accept that the adultery, or some other offense, really did happen. Don't deny it! Only when you face the truth can you move toward forgiveness and resolution.

Emotions

How do we respond emotionally when our spouse commits some wrong against us? When the hurt first comes, we usually have an intense emotional reaction.

When a mate discovers an adulterous affair, it is natural and understandable that emotions run hot. We respond to such an offense with feelings of anger, hurt, grief, even bitterness. And these feelings can lead to a lack of trust in our marriages.

When someone betrays our trust, we feel deep pain; it can take time for those emotions to heal and for trust to be restored. This can be a healthy, normal part of the process of healing and forgiveness. The problem with these feelings is that we can hang on to them indefinitely, often using them as a weapon against the one who hurt us. The use of such weapons always wounds the individual and the relationship.

I know of people who get frozen in place because they refuse to get over the negative emotions and move forward to restore their relationship. Many spouses have told me, "I just can't get over what my husband did to me," or "I'm still hurt and angry for what my wife did years ago." Many of these sad folks hang on to their negative emotions for years, even decades. They become like those who suffer the loss of a loved one, but who can't—or won't—move on and allow healing to take place.

Certainly there is room for an emotional response when your mate has wronged you. The key is knowing what to do with these tormenting emotions.

ARE YOU WILLING TO FORGIVE?

Only rarely have I met someone who declared, "I am completely unwilling to forgive my mate." Most of us automatically say, "Of course, I'm willing to forgive."

But are we, really?

Think back on your life. Can you recall any incidents where you did not extend forgiveness?

Jesus illustrated His command to forgive 490 times with a remarkable parable. He described a servant who owed his king millions of dollars. There was no way in the world that this common laborer could ever repay such a huge debt. Yet he begged the king for more time to get his finances together.

The king had every legal right to throw the man in prison, but he forgave the debt and sent the servant on his way.

You might think that a man shown such tremendous mercy would look for ways to show the same consideration to others. This guy must have felt as light as a feather. But immediately he went looking for a guy who owed him a pittance. He grabbed the man by the throat and shouted, "Pay up!"

The indebted man begged, "Please give me some more time, and I'll pay you back. I just need more time." An oddly familiar request—but instead of showing the man mercy, this servant had his debtor thrown in prison.

"When his fellow slaves saw what happened," Jesus said, "they were deeply grieved and came and reported it to the King."

The ruler reacted with fury. "I forgave you all that debt because you pleaded with me," he said. "Should you not also have had mercy on [the one who owed you]?" (Matthew 18:31–33).

With that, the enraged king issued the order: "Take this ungrateful rascal who wouldn't forgive his friend and throw him into prison. Turn him over to the 'tormentors' until he has paid me every penny back of the huge debt he owes me!" (v. 34, author's paraphrase).

Jesus finished His parable with these chilling words: "My heavenly Father will also do the same to you, if each of you does not forgive his brother from your heart."

Whenever we find ourselves tortured by emotions, we ought to take inventory of whether we have extended forgiveness to those who wronged us. It is *essential* that we forgive those who have hurt us, otherwise we remain locked up in the prison of bitterness and hatred.

TAKING EVERY THOUGHT CAPTIVE

Once we forgive and release old hurts, we need to take another step into freedom by "taking every thought captive" and bringing it into conformity with Jesus Christ and His teaching (2 Corinthians 10:5).

Our minds are battlefields. The enemy of humankind knows that if he can conquer this territory, he can rule the individual. Satan, our adversary, flings damaging thoughts our way; that's his strategy. Such alien thoughts do not belong to the mind of Christ and thus are not compatible with the man or woman who seeks to follow Christ.

Such thoughts take on various disguises. But whether they are immoral, deceitful, angry, lustful, hateful, or selfish, we must treat them all like an invading army and oppose them just as if we were actually soldiers on a battlefield. We attack them and take them captive. They become prisoners of war, and we turn them over to our Commander in Chief, the Lord Jesus Christ. This effectively disarms the invaders and they can no longer threaten us.

The apostle Paul gives us our marching orders: "Let all bitterness and wrath and anger and clamor and slander be put away from you, along with all malice" (Ephesians 4:31). Can you think of a better description of the types of destructive thoughts that need to be taken captive to Christ?

Such thoughts will try one of two methods to attack us: subterfuge or ambush. Sometimes they try to sneak in; at other times they lay in wait as a massive force. Whatever the case, as an act of the will, we must pray something like this: "Father, I'm not going to give any ground to these thoughts by focusing on them. I refuse to let them hold me back or beat up on me. I refuse that suggestion of resentment, of bitterness, of anger and ill will. I turn over all these invading thoughts to the Lord Jesus!"

As we make this a consistent practice, we discover that our emotions gradually come under a greater measure of control —Christ's control.

EXTERNAL CHALLENGES

Punishment

We see our spouse daily, so sometimes it's hard to move beyond the hurt the person caused. As we look at our mate seated across the breakfast table, we might even have the feeling that he or she is getting off too easy. *There needs to be punishment,* we think, *some suffering for the wrong committed against me!*

How do we deal with our feelings toward a person who honestly deserves punishment but whom we are commanded to forgive? It's at this point that we need to remember another biblical principle: Vengeance is the Lord's (e.g., Deuteronomy 32:35; Romans 12:19). Our responsibility is to forgive and to let God take care of any needed discipline or punishment. In His own time, God will balance the scales—for you and me, and for our husbands and wives.

We need to keep this principle in mind when we've been wronged. It will help us to freely extend the forgiveness and mercy that God calls us to give. And it will help us in accomplishing the next step of forgiveness.

Payment

Many of us have little problem in making it to this point in the forgiveness process. Yet even though we know God will handle issues of retribution, a problem still gnaws at us. We want a "little payback" for the wrongs committed against us. It might sound something like this: "I know God will handle the judgment and punishment of my husband. But I want some satisfaction out of all this!"

None of us is perfect; we all need forgiveness and we all need to forgive. So none of us has any right to hold anything against our mates—but we do anyway, don't we? Like the sword of Damocles, we dangle those hurts over our husband's or wife's head, ready to use them whenever we need "leverage."

But the final step in forgiveness requires us to lay down the sword. We need to let those who have hurt us off the hook for what they've done. This means putting the offense behind us and never again seeking repayment or retribution.

Imagine for a moment that you come over to my study and accidentally knock over my favorite lamp. We both look at the floor and see all the shattered pieces, lying everywhere. You can't even tell it used to be a lamp.

You look at me with remorse in your eyes and say, "I'm so sorry! I feel so bad about this. How much did it cost? I'm going to buy you a new one."

As you reach for your wallet, I grab your hand and say, "Hey, don't worry about it. I don't want you to pay for that lamp. In fact, I won't let you pay for it."

What have I done? I've let you off the hook for the offense you committed. But I still need light in my study—so *someone* has to pay for a new lamp. And because I let you off the hook, that someone is going to be me.

Would I have been in the right to allow you to pay for that lamp? Certainly. But instead, I extended mercy to you—in effect, the debt you incurred by breaking my lamp, I declared "paid in full."

All these dynamics must take place if we intend to fully forgive a person.

THE FORGIVENESS CLASSROOM

At the Cross

Where do we learn forgiveness like this? What school do we attend? Our classroom for learning such liberating behavior is the cross of Jesus Christ.

As our Savior hung suspended between earth and heaven, His willing sacrifice made a statement to the world: *"I'll take the punishment you deserve as I die for your sins."* But Jesus went beyond taking the punishment and paid the whole price demanded by our sinful actions. He took the punishment for the condition of sin in *general* and covered the cost for all the things we've shattered by our *individual* sinful actions.

If we are to forgive, we must learn from the example of Christ. First, we must choose to forgive, to close the books on wrongs done to us; this is the role of our will. Second, we must take captive to Christ all those thoughts that try to gnaw away at our decision to forgive; this is the work of our emotions. Third, we must trust God to right the wrongs and balance the books; this is the task of our mind.

Forgiveness: An Act and a Process

Think of the forgiveness process like making a purchase with a credit card. Imagine that you go to a jewelry counter, choose a beautiful diamond bracelet, and slap down the plastic. You sign your name on the receipt . . . and the bracelet is yours. This illustrates the willful *act* of forgiveness.

Then come the monthly payments. Because you bought an expensive bracelet, you have to pay month by month over a long period. So you are both the individual who bought the jewelry *and* the person who continues to pay.

In the same way, forgiveness is both an act and a process. You make a choice at a specific moment in time and the deal is sealed and done. But you choose over time to continue to extend the forgiveness. You make the installments required by your initial decision to forgive.

WHY FORGIVE?

Why should we forgive? I can think of at least four good reasons.

1. God commands us to forgive.

The Bible tells us to "be kind to one another, tender-hearted, forgiving each other, just as God in Christ also has forgiven you" (Ephesians 4:32). I consider this verse so important that I read it to every couple who stands before me at the altar. The truth expressed by this verse contains the secret to every successful marriage and relationship.

2. Forgiveness is part of the character of God.

The Scripture says we should forgive one another just as the Lord forgave us (Colossians 3:13). It is in the very nature of God to forgive—and He does so unconditionally, even when we don't deserve it.

Consider again the credit card illustration. At the cross, God initially extended us credit. Each time we sin against Him and repent, He makes an installment payment to our account. God forgives us 490 times—and much more!

3. Forgiveness is good for us.

Unforgiveness is like adding fertilizer to the "root of bitterness [that springs] up" and defiles everything it touches (Hebrews 12:15), beginning with the individual who harbors the resentment. Unforgiveness can destroy us—literally.

I knew a man who died of various physical ailments at what most of us would consider "middle age." I don't know what the physician wrote down as the cause of death, but it should have been "bitterness." I believe this man died prematurely because he refused to get over many things. He became narrow, negative, and cynical. His "root of bitterness" spread throughout his soul; unforgiveness became the controlling factor in his life. Would forgiveness have healed his mind and body? I have no doubt.

Ironically, the very individuals who have wronged us continue to control us when we refuse to forgive them. Perhaps you know the feeling: You can't forget the individual or the pain he inflicted on you. When you sit down to enjoy a delicious meal, that person sits across the table from you, like a ghost. You find yourself driving down the road, carrying on imagined conversations with that individual, telling him what you wish you could do to him. Or worse, you tell him what you hope God will do to him or where you hope God will send him. His control over you will end only when, through the power of Christ, you forgive that person for the specific wrongs he committed against you.

4. We forgive so that we, too, will be forgiven.

We've all heard it and recited it numerous times, that part of the Lord's Prayer where Jesus teaches us to pray, "Forgive us our debts, as we also have forgiven our debtors" (Matthew 6:12). This single line of the Lord's Prayer says very clearly what the Bible repeatedly teaches concerning forgiveness: If we do not forgive others, God will not forgive us. If you are refusing to forgive your spouse, this biblical fact should send chills down your spine.

You get locked away in a deep and dark emotional and spiritual prison when you refuse to extend forgiveness. To get out of that frightful, suffocating place, you must forgive with your heart, the core of your being. That means when you "bury the hatchet," you burn the map that shows where it's buried!

GOD'S FORGIVENESS: COUNT ON IT

The forgiveness of God seems too good to be true. Whenever I speak on forgiveness, someone almost always asks, "Are you sure God forgave me when I prayed?" Or the person may say, "You know, I don't feel forgiven. Maybe it didn't take."

I always encourage these troubled individuals by reminding them that God is faithful; He keeps His promises. Then I tell them about these various forgiveness promises God has given us.

The first is His "east-west" promise. God removes our sins

from us "as far as the east is from the west" (Psalm 103:12). Now, think about that for a moment. That's an infinite distance, a place found on no map.

Then there's the Lord's "amnesia promise." While it's hard for us to forget, God forgives so thoroughly, He doesn't even remember our sin once we have repented and sought His mercy. "I will forgive their iniquity, and their sin I will remember no more," He declares (Jeremiah 31:34).

Sometimes, we have a hard time releasing others because we keep dredging up our own guilt. We assume that God, who is holy, keeps the record of our sins before Him at all times. But that's simply not the case. When you and I ask God to forgive us for some sinful act or attitude that we previously have confessed to Him, He could easily respond by asking, "What sin are you talking about?" He has forgotten it.

God also has given what I like to refer to as the "stain remover promise." Through Isaiah, the Lord says, "Though your sins are as scarlet, they will be as white as snow" (1:18).

Imagine spilling grape juice on a fresh, white shirt. Only the most effective cleanser can get out such a stain, and even then a hint of purple may linger on the shirt. But when God forgives us, not even the slightest trace of sin's ugly stain remains.

Last, consider God's "deep-sea" promise, recorded by the prophet Micah. God casts "all [our] sins into the depths of the sea" when we repent and receive His forgiveness (7:19). As my precious friend, Corrie ten Boom, always added, not only does He cast our sin into the sea, He puts up a "No Fishing" sign!

Most of us have a difficult time forgiving our mates until we come face-to-face with our own need of God's amazing forgiveness. Once we confront the immensity of grief we have brought to the Father, we begin to understand that the worst offense in a marriage—even adultery—is minor by comparison.

WHAT ABOUT YOU?

The world hums, sings, and even bagpipes the great hymn, "Amazing Grace." Yet how often does it understand the song's rich history?

The British navy compelled the hymn's composer, John Newton, to serve on a ship in 1744. He escaped, was captured, and publicly flogged. At his own request, the navy assigned him to a slave ship. Ultimately, Newton became master of his ship—again, a slave vessel.

On May 10, 1748, his frail craft plowed through a massive storm. Newton felt sure the ship would sink and cried out to God for mercy. When the rain and wind subsided, Newton returned to his cabin and considered the irony of asking for mercy when he had a hold full of chained human beings, stolen from their homeland and destined, via his ship, for the slave market.

Overwhelmed at his own unworthiness, Newton realized that God had extended to him a grace, an unearned, undeserved favor that could be described only as "amazing."

What about you? What is your "amazing grace" story? When we realize the amazing scope of God's forgiveness, we will find the strength to forgive our mate 490 times . . . *and more.*

REFLECTING ON YOUR RELATIONSHIP

1. In what specific areas of marriage do you have the most trouble obeying Jesus' command to forgive "seventy times seven" times?

2. List some of the "little foxes" that you need to forgive.

3. What usually blocks your willingness to forgive?

4. Why would God, who is perfect in holiness, allow you into His heaven, even though you have wronged Him with your sin?

A PERSONAL WORD
Thou Shalt Keep the Home Fires Burning

Your love will mature, but the sizzle should go on and on. If not, something is wrong with you! This commandment is the secret to romancing the home.

—E. Y.

Commandment 8

THOU SHALT KEEP
THE HOME FIRES BURNING

O ne of my top goals in life is to have a happy marriage."
That's the reply the average American gives again and
again to pollsters who ask what he or she wants out of life.
Although we were never "polled," Jo Beth and I certainly had
that as our top goal when we married more than four decades
ago. I'll never forget that day. Her uncle, now deceased, performed our wedding ceremony. Holding us both in a steady
gaze, he quoted these words from poet Robert Browning:

Grow old along with me!
The best is yet to be,
The last of life, for which the first was made:
Our times are in His hand
Who saith "A whole I planned,
Youth shows but half; trust God: see all, nor be afraid!"[1]

I believe that every man and woman standing at the altar wants to believe, "The best is yet to be." In order for those words to become reality, though, we must be able to say honestly to our mate, "Grow old along with me." And the best way to make sure that happens is to keep the home fires burning.

MARRIAGE MEANS WORK

Contrary to what many folks think, best wishes and good luck have nothing to do with the health and happiness of a marriage. A good marriage results from working hard and by putting the timeless principles of God's Word at the center of the relationship. Marital happiness really is a matter of choice. It comes when we do the things that keep our love growing and maturing—even during the tough times that surely will come.

This idea forms the basis of my eighth commandment of marriage: *Thou shalt keep the home fires burning.*

Marriage is seldom an easy proposition. At some point, every marriage sees an end to the honeymoon bliss. Even so, the end of the honeymoon need not mean the end of happiness or passion. Every married couple can keep the fires of love burning long after the honeymoon has become nothing but a sweet memory. How can we do that? That's the topic of this chapter. First, let's meet a couple who remind us of the need to work at our marriage.

A MARRIAGE MADE IN HEAVEN

True Love Story

In an era when men and women married at very young ages, Isaac had passed his fortieth birthday before he even met Rebekah. Why did it take Isaac so long to find "the right one"? Because he had determined to obey God, whatever the cost.

Isaac lived in a pagan area where, as we say in Texas, there were slim pickins'. True, all kinds of women lived all around, but Isaac knew better than to marry outside his faith. He wanted a woman who shared his trust in the one true God, and he refused to settle for anything less. If he couldn't find such a woman right away, he would remain single. And that's the way things stood for many years.

After Isaac's mother, Sarah, died, Abraham took it upon himself to change his son's marital status. In line with the custom of that day, Abraham commissioned one of his trusted servants to find Isaac a wife: "I will make you swear by the LORD, the God of heaven and the God of earth, that you shall not take a wife for my son from the daughters of the Canaanites, among whom I live, but you will go to my country and to my relatives, and take a wife for my son Isaac" (Genesis 24:3–4).

So the faithful servant set out to find a bride for Isaac. The servant obeyed his master's orders to the letter, going to extraordinary lengths to make certain he found just the right woman. At last he encountered a charming, beautiful shepherdess, and after getting acquainted with her, he had no doubt that God had chosen her to be the wife of his master's son.

Isaac waited for many months—maybe even a year or two—for the servant to return with his bride. With the following words Scripture describes one of the most romantic moments in biblical history:

> Isaac went out to meditate in the field toward evening; and he lifted up his eyes and looked and behold, camels were coming. Rebekah lifted up her eyes, and when she saw Isaac she dismounted from the camel. She said to the servant, "Who is that man walking in the field to meet us?" And the servant said, "He is my master." Then she took her veil and covered herself. The servant told Isaac all the things that he had done. Then Isaac brought her into his mother Sarah's tent, and he took Rebekah, and she became his wife, and he loved her. (vv. 63–67)

A romantic story? You bet! But it's also the story of a godly man waiting on the Lord to work out the details of his marriage. Isaac had the faith it took to believe that God would bring the right person to the right place at the right time. He and his family had prayed about his need and refused to compromise. The result speaks for itself: "And he loved her."

Like Every Marriage

When we consider how this marriage began, it seems impossible that the relationship could be anything but perfect. Yet problems soon arose and then multiplied. By the end of Genesis 27—after years of marriage and several children—duplicity, competition, antagonism, tension, and anger had elbowed their way into Isaac's family.

This biblical account of a "match made in heaven" illustrates what every married couple needs to remember. Even marriages with the best of beginnings *will* have their share of problems. Over time, a brightly burning fire of love can fade and smolder; if we are careless, it can flicker out altogether. Unless a husband and wife work hard to keep the fire alive, they can wake up one morning to find the warm breezes replaced by an arctic breeze howling through their bedroom.

THREE STAGES OF MARRIAGE

How can a couple keep their marriage from freezing over? How can they keep the fires of love and passion burning?

Well, how do you keep *any* fire burning? You work at it. You feed it, tend it, and encourage it. Neglect it, and it will soon burn itself out.

The same thing is true of marriage. It takes work. But if you'll persevere and faithfully apply God's principles to your marriage, you can enjoy a growing and exciting relationship.

Success in fire building, whether in marriage or at the campground, also depends on understanding how fires burn over time and what they require at every stage. With that in mind, let's take a brief look at three key stages of the marriage fire.

1. The Honeymoon Stage

Nearly every married couple has passed through the honeymoon stage. During this stage your mate can do no wrong and you simply can't get enough of one another. The honeymoon stage abounds with moonlight and roses, violins and candlelight. The fire burns bright and hot, and you bask in its warm glow. It's a wonderful time.

As we've seen, the Song of Solomon offers the most romantic, erotic imagery in all of Scripture. It describes perfectly what goes on between a husband and a wife during the honeymoon stage, when each focuses on and delights in the other person. Consider the passion that Solomon and his wife shared:

> [He:] "Like a lily among the thorns, so is my darling among the maidens."
>
> [She:] "Like an apple tree among the trees of the forest, so is my beloved among the young men. In his shade I took great delight and sat down, and his fruit was sweet to my taste. He has brought me to his banquet hall, and his banner over me is love. Sustain me with raisin cakes, refresh me with apples, because I am lovesick." . . .
>
> [He:] "O my dove, in the clefts of the rock, in the secret place of the steep pathway, let me see your form, let me hear your voice; for your voice is sweet, and your form is lovely." . . .
>
> [She:] "My beloved is mine, and I am his; He pastures his flock among the lilies. Until the cool of the day when the shadows flee away, turn, my beloved, and be like a gazelle or a young stag on the mountains of Bether." (2:2–5, 14, 16–17)

Solomon's love song pictures two people who spend all their time together reveling in one another and all their time apart longing to come together again. Their passion burns white-hot, consuming the young couple without burning them up. They want nothing more than each other. They feel completely taken with one another on all levels: physically, emotionally, and spiritually.

Idealism colors the passion of the honeymoon stage. Both partners believe the other to be perfect in every way: "You are altogether beautiful, my darling, and there is no blemish in you" (4:7). No more flawless a creature exists than the object of honeymoon-stage love. He's everything a man could be and she fully embodies feminine perfection. Both parties seem blinded to any flaws or defects in the other. They want only to hold hands, to look into one another's eyes, and to make love, day and night.

One writer described a friend living in the honeymoon stage:

> She honestly claims that the sky is bluer; she's noticed the delicate fragrance of the lilacs beside her garage, though she previously walked past them without stopping; and Mozart moves her to tears. In short, life has never been so exciting. "I'm young again!" she shouts exuberantly. I have to admit, the guy must be better than Weight Watchers. She has lost 15 pounds and looks like a cover girl. She's taken a new interest in the shape of her thighs.[2]

Yet this stage doesn't last forever (as hard as that may be for those in its grip to believe). The second stage of marital love occurs at roughly the same time that reality sets in.

2. The Party's Over Stage

In "the party's over" stage, a couple truly gets to know one another. Reality sets in and both partners begin to see one another's true humanity, with all its flaws and imperfections.

Many couples feel traumatized at the dawning of this stage. A little "buyer's remorse" may even set in: She begins to question if he's really the man she thought she married, while he wonders what happened to the sweet, lovely young thing he couldn't get enough of during their first years of marriage. Counselor Kay Kuzma writes that "for most of us, our wedding day was one of the highlights of our lives. But the honeymoon is soon over, and our courtship dreams of romance and candlelight too often dissolve into the reality of dirty dishes and diapers."[3]

If you've been married for any length of time, you've been here. Even Solomon, the hot-blooded young writer of the Song of Solomon, reached this stage. The same man who wrote of his young wife's perfection later wrote, "A constant dripping on a day of steady rain and a contentious woman are alike. He who would restrain her restrains the wind, and grasps oil with his right hand"(Proverbs 27:15–16). And on what must have been an even bleaker day, he penned the acidic words, "I find more bitter than death the woman who is a snare, whose heart is a trap and whose hands are chains. The man who pleases God will escape her, but the sinner she will ensnare" (Ecclesiastes 7:26 NIV).

It's hard to find a pleasant mental image anywhere in those harsh statements! Imagine trying to sleep while listening to the constant *drip, drip, drip* of heavy rain on the roof. Or ponder trying to go about your business with your feet in a snare, your heart tied in knots, and your wrists handcuffed together. That's the word picture Solomon paints of a husband who realizes the party's over.

Of course, not all marital unhappiness can be laid at the feet of nagging or contemptuous wives. Far from it!

"Bob acted very differently now than he did during their courtship and early months of marriage," one Christian psychologist wrote. Once,

173

Bob was spontaneous and attentive. [Geri] loved the times of deep sharing of their hopes, dreams, fears and feelings. But after a year of marriage, things began to change. Bob became more and more interested in his new job and less and less attentive to Geri. Their long talks became five-minute "quickies"— more an exchange of information than deep dialogue. When Geri confronted him with this, he said she was being too sensitive. He loved her just as much as before; it was just that he was trying to show his boss that he could be counted on and that he was physically tired.[4]

At this stage of marriage, a couple must make a choice. At least three options lay open to husbands and wives who realize the party's over.

First, they may adopt an attitude of glum resignation, determined to stick it out in the hope that something will happen. They live under the same roof in misery, trying hard to keep up the appearance of a happy union. They feel bored with each other, angry at each other, hostile toward each other, or indifferent toward each other—but because of the children or because they don't believe in divorce, they remain together.

Second, they may opt for divorce. Far too many couples that get to the party's over stage become disillusioned with one another and choose to bail out.

But there is good news! No couple needs to choose between living together in misery or ending their marriage. A third option exists. A couple who chooses this option decides not just to stay together but to do whatever it takes to make their marriage genuinely happy and healthy.

3. The Best Is Yet to Be Stage

Couples who resolve to get through the party's over stage move on to the most exciting and rewarding stage of all, the best is yet to be.

This stage stands against the old saying that "love is blind." This love—mature love—is anything *but* blind. It sees everything in its beloved, all the character flaws and imperfections and quirks, yet can't help but shower the spouse with words and deeds of affection and love. Nothing can kill this love. This kind of love can endure anything, even the radical changes that spouses sometimes undergo after years of marriage.

In the year he celebrated his fiftieth wedding anniversary, the late Bible scholar Kenneth S. Kantzer wrote a magazine column in *Christianity Today*, entitled, "The Freedom of Jealousy." There is great wisdom in his words:

> My wife is 75 years old. At times her face is etched with "old-age wrinkles" (or so she calls them), and, true to her femininity, she hates them.
>
> On the other hand, I think the lines are beautiful, and I love every one of them. I tell her they may come with advancing years, but they are lines of character—not old-age wrinkles. And I remind her of a bumper sticker a friend of mine reported seeing: "If you is fifty and ain't got no wrinkles, you ain't smiled enough."
>
> This is the fiftieth year of our marriage and, yes, we are still in love. Our love is more intellectual—more understanding—than it was 50 years ago. It is also deeper and stronger—though no less ardent. It is, in fact, a jealous love, and that is the way it should be. After all, God is jealous (Exodus 20:5 and Deuteronomy 5:9). He wants us to love only Him as our God. But that does not stifle our love for others. Just the reverse! It frees us to love others.
>
> So it is with our love as husband and wife. It gives all and demands all, yet does not impinge upon the love each of us has for God. Nor does it lessen our love for our son and daughter, their spouses, our grandchildren, friends, and so on. The more you love, the more you can love. . . .
>
> Fifty years is a long time for two people to live together. But

for us, each year is better than the one before. And we are thankful to God.[5]

Anyone can enjoy the best is yet to be stage, so long as he or she applies some basic biblical principles to their marriage. And best of all, the mature love of this stage offers more genuine excitement and true romance per square inch than the honeymoon stage. Any husband or wife can happily look at a spouse of five, ten, fifteen, or more years—even half a century—and honestly say, "I am so happy we get to grow old together!"

THE LOOK OF MATURE LOVE

I wish I could tell you that my many wonderful years of marriage to Jo Beth have given me the ability to demonstrate what mature love really looks like. But I could live another thousand years and still never top the Word of God when it comes to giving a picture of mature love.

Read God's definition of mature love found in the famous "Love Chapter," 1 Corinthians 13:

> Love is patient, love is kind and is not jealous; love does not brag and is not arrogant, does not act unbecomingly; it does not seek its own, is not provoked, does not take into account a wrong suffered, does not rejoice in unrighteousness, but rejoices with the truth; bears all things, believes all things, hopes all things, endures all things. Love never fails. (vv. 4–8)

I love the simplicity of this passage. In many ways, it gives us a detailed explanation of our Lord's words, "Treat others the same way you want them to treat you" (Luke 6:31).

How would you rate your love for your spouse? Are you stuck in one of the first two stages of marital love, or is your love maturing? I encourage you to do what I like to do from time to time—use 1 Corinthians 13 as a personal checklist.

Mature Love Is . . .

❑ Patient. I put up with the imperfections of my mate.

❑ Kind. I perform acts of kindness for the other person.

❑ Joyful with truth. My love grows out of a base of honesty and integrity.

❑ Trusting. I believe in the best from my spouse.

❑ Full of hope. I hope for the best from and for my mate.

❑ Enduring. My love lasts through even the toughest of times.

Mature Love Is Not . . .

❑ Jealous. Instead, it rests secure.

❑ Boastful. Instead, it refrains from building itself up.

❑ Arrogant. Instead, it humbles itself.

❑ Self-seeking. Instead, it puts a spouse's needs and desires first.

❑ Angry. Instead, it refrains from rash outbursts.

❑ Looking for paybacks. Instead, mature love forgives, even when treated wrongly.

But Most of All . . .

❑ Love never fails! I'm always there to support my spouse.

WORKING TOWARD A MATURE LOVE

Mature love can withstand every trial thrown its way. It lasts throughout the years—but only through choosing to do the work necessary to make it grow. Consider some basic principles that can help your love grow into the mature love you desire. Put them into practice and the best will be yet to come!

1. Speak blessings.

The first basic principle is *speak up*. Speak words of blessing to your partner, and do it consistently.

Far too often, words flow from our mouths with little thought behind them. We can say things that hurt our husband or wife before we realize it. Maybe you're not like me, but I find that hurtful remarks come pretty naturally, while the positive ones take more thought. The Bible tells us the tongue is the toughest muscle in our body to control. "With it we bless our Lord and Father, and with it we curse men, who have been made in the likeness of God; from the same mouth come both blessing and cursing" (James 3:9–10).

Some couples fall into the bad habit of belittling one another in the presence of others. They cut one another down, encouraged by laughter, firing off one-liners about what a mate said, how he sounds and looks, how much she eats or spends money. They make the party circuit like a traveling road show, making jokes and insults about their husband or wife that would make Don Rickles sound like an amateur.

This can become the equivalent of speaking curses to one another. The couple may laugh and appear to be good sports at first—but after a while, such behavior gets old. If someone constantly makes put-downs about me, I begin to wonder if that's not the way he *really* feels toward me.

The best way to bury a marriage is for a husband and wife to keep digging at one another. Instead, we need to speak blessings to our marriage partner. Even if you do not practice put-down humor, become proactive and practice affirming comments and compliments that encourage your spouse. We need to bestow God's blessing on each other.

The word *blessing* comes from a combination of three terms: *will*, *well*, and *word*. So to speak a blessing on our husband or wife, we speak a *willing word* and a *well word*. This produces healing and soothes any scars brought on by conflict. When blessing marks the pattern of communication between a husband and wife, the marriage moves forward into the mature love stage.

Psychologist Nathaniel Branden has studied the habits of couples who have been happily married for many years. He highlights nine ways in which husbands and wives can keep their love alive. Guess what he lists first?

"My own studies," he writes, "as well as those of other marriage counselors, show that happy couples consistently . . . say, *'I love you.'* Happy couples express their love in words. They do not say, 'What do you mean, do I love you? I married you, didn't I?' 'Saying the words,' one woman remarked, 'is a way of touching.'"[6]

If we want marriages that not only go the distance but also get better year after year, then we need to learn how to effectively show our appreciation for our spouses. Train yourself to *speak up* words of blessing and approval. Make sure that your words to and about your partner—in private and in the company of others—affirm, praise, build up, and heal. Speak positive words to one another . . . and watch the flames between you grow hotter with every blessing you toss on the fire.

2. Open up and confess.

The popular 1970 movie *Love Story,* based on the equally popular novel by Erich Segal, had one famous line that cropped up everywhere—on bumper stickers, posters, newspaper columns—and worse, it became the conventional wisdom of young people in love. The line? "Love means never having to say you're sorry."

That statement drives me crazy! Nothing could be further from the truth. Love means having to say you're sorry . . . a lot! Mature love drives the husband to ask forgiveness of his wife every time he realizes he's hurt her in any way. Mature love compels a wife to say, "I'm sorry," and make amends whenever she sees she has wounded her husband.

The apostle James put it this way: "Therefore, confess your sins to one another, and pray for one another so that you may be healed" (James 5:16). We usually interpret this verse with regard to a sick human body. The principle can also apply, however, to an ailing marriage. If you want a marriage that burns brighter through the years, then *open up* and confess your sins to one another.

To move a marriage to the best is yet to be stage of mature love, a man and woman must admit their wrong actions. So often they spend their passion in trying to "win" their marital battles. But always having to be right is a sign of immaturity; maturity is the ability to concede a mistake, seek forgiveness, and move on.

Confession that heals wounds gets specific about the offenses committed. It may sound something like this:

- "I'm sorry that I didn't pay attention to you earlier when you tried to tell me about your mother."
- "Please forgive me for replying with those sarcastic words."
- "I apologize for not consulting you before I bought the chair."

All kinds of great things happen when we humble ourselves and confess our specific sins, both to God and to our spouse. Lines of communication open up. Healing takes place, even the healing of long-festering wounds. Best of all, when we confess our faults to one another, we draw closer to God, who then pours out His forgiveness and blessings on our marriage.

3. Change yourself, not your mate.

Far too many couples start at the *altar* and then proceed to *alter!* Something about human nature makes us want to correct, improve, change, repair, and revise the people around us. But in marriage, this "drive to revise" can cause major problems.

It took ten years of marriage to convince Elizabeth Cody Newenhuyse that she couldn't change her man into the vision enshrined in her brain. "Admit it," she writes. "We've all tried to change our husbands. But after 10 years I've finally wised up. . . . Fritz went to Harvard, but he never learned that liquid spills become *solid* spills if not wiped immediately. I've tried educating him. I've yelled, I've cajoled, I've even gotten out the SOS pad and scrubbed. No change. I've decided it's a basic hormonal difference: Men don't scrub stoves, because they literally don't see the spill. So rather than nag, I quietly wipe."[7]

Big problems arise when we believe that it's our job to change the one we married. Maybe the wife believes she can change her husband and make him into a more organized, "neater" person, or the husband thinks he can change his wife into a more passionate lover. The result is usually frustration— or worse.

I don't know who told us that it's our job to change the people around us, but we have to give up that idea—especially in our marriages. We must stop trying to shame and manipulate our mates into being what we want them to be. And we have to stop asking God to change our mates into our own vision of perfection.

I am responsible to change just one person, and that's Ed Young. (And in reality the Changer does that!) It's not my job and it's not your job to change anyone but ourselves. It's not even my job to change Jo Beth or our three sons and their families. Accept your husband or wife unconditionally and let God work on any necessary changes.

Years ago I heard the story of Dorothy Payne's marriage to a fellow she nicknamed Jimmy; he called her Dolly. Dolly, twenty years younger than Jimmy and quite plump, loved to dress in loud colors. At social occasions, Dolly always grabbed center stage; everyone knew her as the life of the party. Jimmy, on the other hand, took everything very seriously. His thoughtful and scholarly approach made him a classic introvert. Instead of dressing in bright, stylish colors, he dressed like a mortician going to his own funeral.

Yet in their marriage, neither Dolly nor Jimmy tried to change the other. He added gravity to her effervescent personality, while she brought a sense of fun to his reserved nature. When once questioned about a decision her husband had made, Dolly simply said, "I would hope my husband is always right, but right or wrong, he's my husband." Because they did not try to change each other, they enjoyed a beautiful relationship. In fact, she felt extremely happy to be married to her Jimmy—our James Madison, fourth president of the United States.

THE MAKING OF A *MATURE* MARRIAGE

As you move toward developing a mature marital love, consider the following six pointers. The acronym *MATURE* may help you to lay a solid foundation for the work required to enjoy a fulfilling marriage. To become mature, be . . .

1. **M**otivated. No one completes anything worthwhile without proper motivation. It takes hard work to build a marriage and in order to find the energy required, you must find the motivation within yourself. But that shouldn't be hard. Do you want a happy, long-lasting marriage? Do you want to please and bless God? Do you want to provide an attractive example of what Christ can do in

a human heart? When you remind yourself often of the goal and the reward, you'll find the motivation.

2. **A**ttentive. Attentiveness is the key to any good marriage, just as inattentiveness is a symptom of an unhealthy one. Pay attention to your mate's thoughts, feelings, and needs. Become a student of your spouse. Carefully note his or her likes and dislikes, strengths and weaknesses, pet peeves and personal delights. Note them and then act on them. No one can put the spark back in a marriage and move into the third stage of marriage without developing habits of attentiveness.

3. **T**ender. The apostle Paul tells us to be "tender-hearted" (Ephesians 4:32). Any man who wants a successful marriage must learn to be tender with his wife. At the same time, even the biggest, toughest, and roughest man needs tenderness from his wife. So go out of your way to find creative methods of demonstrating tenderness— and use them every day.

4. **U**nderstanding. In order to understand our husbands or wives, we need to practice our third marriage commandment. Remember it? "Thou shalt *continually* communicate." Effective communication between men and women takes work, but it can flourish. And it's the key to understanding our mates—grasping how they speak, the nonverbal signs and signals they project, and how they respond to what we communicate. Reach beyond your own limited understanding and figure out how your mate is wired. But if you skip this essential step, you won't reach the best is yet to be stage.

5. **R**espectful. Everyone wants to feel respected, to know that his or her opinions and thoughts are valued by another, particularly by a spouse. Ephesians 5 suggests a sort of reverence between a husband and wife, a respect that goes much deeper than in other relationships.

Submitting to one another out of respect, of course, doesn't always mean that two people agree. It does mean, however, that the two honor one another, even when they don't see eye to eye. Such respect gives husbands and wives the ability to submit to one another.

6. Excited. The best is yet to be stage can provide even more excitement than the first months of the honeymoon stage. I can personally testify that no part of my marriage has felt any more exciting or fulfilling than the current stage of mature love that Jo Beth and I are working on. When you can say, "Our time now is much more exciting and fulfilling. I love growing older and seeing our love get stronger every day we are together," yours is a mature love. Such love grows and matures only with time and effort.

GROW OLD ALONG WITH ME

We all want a "best is yet to be" marriage, one in which our love will grow and last. With that in mind, let me quote a stanza found a little later in Browning's poem "Rabbi Ben Ezra." We didn't read this portion at our wedding, but Jo Beth and I are making it part of our marriage. I recommend that you do too.

Not once beat "Praise be Thine!
I see the whole design,
I, who saw power, see now love perfect too:
Perfect I call Thy plan:
Thanks that I was a man!
Maker, remake, complete,—I trust what Thou shalt do!

REFLECTING ON YOUR RELATIONSHIP

1. How important is it to you to "work" in making your marriage a happy, passionate, loving one? Explain.

2. In what stage of marriage are you today? What steps do you need to take to move on to the next stage?

3. Do you consider your marriage a loving, passionate one now? Explain. What can you do to make it so?

4. In what areas of MATURE love are you strong? Explain. Where are you weak, and what can you do about it, starting today?

A PERSONAL WORD
Thou Shalt Begin Again and Again

If you have not discovered the thrill of beginning again, you are missing a basic building block of marriage! If your marriage is boring or routine, you need this chapter desperately. Read between the lines and you will be amazed at the change that will take place in you and your spouse.

—E. Y.

THOU SHALT BEGIN AGAIN AND AGAIN

In the summer of 2000, the CBS television network introduced America to a new style of programming, "reality TV."
The groundbreaking show *Survivor* pitted sixteen men and
women against one another and nature on a deserted island
in the South China Sea.

Participants in that and subsequent editions of the series
were challenged to outwit, outplay, and outlast each other as
they hacked out their relationships—as well as dense bamboo.
They had to build shelter, find food, and manage to exist in the
unforgiving environment of a handpicked remote location
(kept secret to provide suspense).

Although successful contestants had to work cooperatively,
each week they would gather at a "tribal council" to vote off
the weakest contestant. Ultimately, one survivor won a million
dollars (and usually a guest appearance on David Letterman's
Late Show).

Although the action on *Survivor* always comes to an end, there is one "survival" series that never ends. It's called *marriage*.

Like the stars of *Survivor,* a husband and wife have to hack out their relationship in a hostile environment. And while the average couple doesn't have to make a life on a wild and deserted island off Borneo, they do have to establish a home in an adversarial climate that often does not treat kindly either marriage or the family.

SURVIVAL RATE

Imagine that we joined a group of tourists heading toward Disney World. Each of us drives our own car. But prior to leaving, we are told that half the cars in our group will be involved in accidents that will dramatically affect the rest of our lives.

Wouldn't you drive with extreme caution? I would. I would ban all cell phone calls, never think of reaching around to find my favorite tape or CD, and pull off the highway at the first sign of drowsiness. I would take time to map out my route and choose the safest way possible. I would do everything in my power to make sure I didn't end up in the wrong half of that 50 percent statistic.

Good news: The statistic does not apply to visitors headed for Disney World. So have a great, safe trip! Bad news: It *does* apply to marriages. Statisticians tell us that half those who say, "I do," in America are headed for a marital wreck. Tragically, almost the same rate holds true for those who profess to be Christians.

I believe, without question, the number one problem in our country today is divorce. When the foundational relationship in the home comes apart, it scars not only the couple but the children, the in-laws, the grandparents, friends, even the church. You'd be hard-pressed to name one of society's ills that can't be traced to the breakdown of the family. Is it any wonder that God says He hates divorce (Malachi 2:16)?

What's the secret to survival? I believe the answer is in our ninth marriage commandment: *Thou shalt begin again and again.*

Our God is the God of a second chance. He begins every day by renewing His mercies to us. The prophet Jeremiah had witnessed unspeakable sufferings and horrors when he wrote, "Because of the LORD's great love we are not consumed, for his compassions never fail. They are *new every morning;* great is your faithfulness" (Lamentations 3:22–23 NIV, italics added).

This is one of the things I love and appreciate most about our God. He is a God who redeems, who delights in taking what was damaged, hurting, and left for dead and making it new, alive, and growing. In short, He is a God who renews.

You would be hard-pressed to find many long-lasting marriages where one or both partners aren't grateful for the opportunity to "begin again." We're human, and so are our mates. But if we're willing to do what it takes, there is nothing from which our marriages can't recover.

SOME FAULTY FOUNDATIONS

From a human perspective, we can't call too many marriages "a match made in heaven." I believe that most marriages start with some sort of problem, conflict, or deception. Many marriages begin with terrible strife between the two families, with two immature people who don't seem to have much in common, or even an unplanned pregnancy.

Perhaps you have found yourself thinking of some couple: *Those two don't have a chance! I give it a year, two at the most.* I must admit, I've seen couples headed for the altar and wondered if they have any idea how difficult marriage can be, even for the most loving, caring couples.

In my forty-plus years as a pastor, I've heard just about every reason or excuse possible from disgruntled spouses as to why their marriages are not making it. Most of the reasons have to do with a faulty beginning:

- "She doesn't like any of my friends!"
- "We got off to a bad start because we didn't have the kind of wedding I wanted."
- "He never got along with my mother and father. I thought that would change, but it just got worse!"
- "When we were dating, we seemed to have so much in common. Now he doesn't like any of the things I like!"
- "She was so sweet when we dated. Now all she does is boss me around!"
- "He never says or does anything romantic anymore!"

During courtship, we all tend to "put our best foot forward." It only makes sense. We look our best, dress our best, even think and behave considerately. We do all these things to give our dates the idea that this is who we were before we met, who we are now, and who we will be after years of marriage. We want that "significant other" to think they've landed a great catch.

What deception!

I'm not suggesting, of course, that we intentionally set out to deceive. Most of us head into marriage with the best and most honorable of intentions. But when you live year after year with the same person, it's inevitable that the "real you" eventually emerges. And when it does, the sight isn't always pretty.

In a nineteenth-century best-selling book titled *The Royal Path of Life*, authors T. L. Haines and L. W. Yaggy claimed that "courtship is a grand scheme of deception." Eventually reality sets in, when "every day reveals something new and something unpleasant. The courtship character fades away, and with it the courtship love. Now comes disappointment, sorrow, regret. They find that their characters are entirely dissimilar."[1]

A deceptive foundation can certainly get a marriage off to

a shaky start. But even so, don't throw up your hands and give up on your mate, your marriage, or yourself. You can begin again in your marriage, no matter how faulty its foundation.

Later in this chapter I will suggest some practical steps to help you begin anew in your marriage. First, however, let's take a look at one marriage that had a shaky—to say the least! —beginning.

A "NO CHANCE" MARRIAGE

The Great Deceiver

The Bible gives us a stark picture of a marriage that most people would say had no chance of survival. The bride was not the groom's first choice. In fact, she wasn't even a close second! Besides that, the marriage started in deception.

A man named Jacob starred in this shaky romance. Just to give you an idea of what kind of guy "Big Jake" was, his name means "one who supplants." In Texas we'd prefer the synonym "cheater"! This con artist had fleeced his brother out of his inheritance by tricking his own father. He developed a reputation as some kind of "wheeler-dealer." (See Genesis 27 for an account of his dealings with his father and brother.)

Jacob fell "head over heels" for Rachel the first time he saw her. The Bible says he kissed her the first time they met and he knew she was "the one"! So Jacob approached Rachel's father, Laban, who also happened to be Jacob's uncle. In Laban, Jacob met his match—a man as smooth and every bit as sly as a fox. Laban decided to get his money's worth out of ol' Jake. So when Jacob asked Laban for Rachel's hand in marriage, the old fox replied, "If you want my daughter Rachel, you'll have to work for me for seven years."

No problem for Jacob! The Bible says Jacob loved Rachel so much that the seven years "seemed to him but a few days" (Genesis 29:20). He worked hard for Laban day after day, month after month, and year after year. Whenever he got tired or discouraged, he must have looked over and seen his lovely bride-to-be and gained renewed energy. Time seemed to fly!

Finally the wedding day arrived—a huge celebration with music and dancing and laughter and wine. Jacob noted the beautiful bride and the proud parents, giggling sisters and nieces and prankish brothers and nephews. And the wine flowed. Apparently Jacob drank a lot of it.

No doubt a little dizzy from the wine, Jacob and his bride retreated for their wedding night to consummate the marriage. The next morning, Jacob awoke, probably trying to rub from his eyes the blur of the night's festivities and erase his hangover. He squinted in the direction of his beloved, whom he could now see clearly in the morning light. Jacob did a double take. It was not Rachel but Leah, her sister!

He had been conned! So now the cheater had become the cheated.

Jacob jumped up from the mat, tugged on his tunic, and bolted out the tent in search of Laban.

"What have you done to me?" Jacob asked his grinning father-in-law. "I worked seven years to earn Rachel's hand in marriage, and you tricked me!"

"Oh, by the way," answered Laban, "there was something I forgot to mention."

Jacob stared at Laban.

"It's not our custom around here to marry off the younger before the firstborn. Tell you what I'm gonna do. Work for me another seven years, and I'll give you Rachel right now." (Read the actual account in Genesis 29:21–28.)

Poor Beginnings

So Jacob wound up with two wives. But wait; the situation quickly got even more complicated. Laban gave both Leah and Rachel handmaids, so Bilhah and Zilpah entered the picture.

And Jacob found himself in a household with two wives and their two maids.

Can you imagine a marriage with a poorer beginning?

The story continues. Apparently Jacob did not love Leah because her "eyes were weak" (v. 17). That doesn't mean she wore bifocals but that the girl had no spark in her eyes—no chemistry. Apparently Leah was pretty dull and uninteresting. Even her name means "cow"; need we say more?

But Rachel *had it!* The Bible describes her as shapely and beautiful. She had zip, glow, charisma, and chemistry.

Nevertheless, Leah began to bear children for Jacob—four boys in succession. This turn of events troubled Rachel. So far she had not been able to bear a child. So she decided to try another way.

In accordance with the customs of that day, she brought Zilpah, her handmaid, to Jacob, who became pregnant with his child. As soon as the infant was born, he was placed on Rachel's knees and becomes for all practical purposes her own. In time Zilpah has another son for Rachel, who can now say to Leah, "I'm catching up with you; I have as much prestige with Jacob as you!" (author's paraphrase; see Genesis 30:1–8).

Let's look at what happens next. Leah becomes worried; she has not gotten pregnant for a while. She figures that what works for Rachel will work for her. So she sends for her handmaid, Bilhah, and presents *her* to Jacob. Bilhah conceives and gives birth to a son, then to another.

So now Jacob is living with four women—four unhappy, competing, bickering women. Leah cheers up a bit when she becomes pregnant once more. She has a son, then another, and later gives birth to a daughter as well.

Whew! I think we need to call "time-out." I'm willing to bet that no one, not even with the most cynical sense of humor, could come up with a more dysfunctional scenario than this.

Even in our day, when the whole idea of marriage and family has grown confused and mixed up, it's hard to imagine a worse start to marriage than Jacob's. The reason? This marriage began on a foundation of deception, and deception poisons a marriage from the outset.

This would be enough to cause headaches for any man, but it wasn't the only problem in Jacob's dysfunctional household. Don't forget the power struggle! Two wives and two concubines competed for the prestige of bearing children, an honor greatly treasured in that culture. They went at it tooth and nail, vying with one another for supremacy.

OVERCOMING BAD BEGINNINGS

Would you find it surprising that this marriage that began in such a lousy manner actually had a terrific ending? We get a clue when the Bible tells us that Rachel grew jealous of Leah (30:1).

Rachel, jealous of Leah? The woman Jacob loved so passionately and wanted to marry in the first place, jealous of the one the Bible says he did not love?

Evidently, something developed between Jacob and Leah. When Jacob decided to move his family, flocks, and household possessions back to his homeland of Canaan, he talked it over with Rachel *and* Leah (31:4). This provides evidence that Leah, who had not been Jacob's favorite, was gaining prominence in the eyes of her husband.

But what really shows the development of the relationship between Jacob and Leah comes at a time of death. Rachel died during a family journey and Jacob buried her by the side of the road near Bethlehem. But when Leah died, Jacob buried her in the Cave of Machpelah, the family plot, a place of honor —where Abraham and Sarah lay, along with Isaac and Rebekah. Jacob, too, would be buried there when he died. Jacob could have arranged for Rachel's body to be relocated to this chosen burial spot, but he never did. The place beside him in death belonged to Leah.

Most significant, it was through Leah—the woman Jacob was tricked into marrying—and not Rachel that the Messiah would come. Through the lineage of Judah, the son of Jacob and Leah, Christ came into this world.

The marriage that began so terribly finished strong! The story of Jacob, Leah, and Rachel demonstrates an important principle: *Bad beginnings are not decisive in a marriage.* No matter how badly our marriages may have begun, they can finish strong if we allow God to heal and renew them.

SIX PRINCIPLES FOR
BEGINNING AGAIN AND AGAIN

If the formula for marital happiness could be found in a pill, it might be "Vitamin A." The following elements of restoration, or beginning again, all begin with the letter "A" and are based on the Scriptures listed with them.[2] We keep coming back to the Bible, don't we? That's because God's way works—in marriage and in all of life! Therefore, the faithful application of biblical principles can bring new life and vitality to any marriage, no matter what its condition. That includes yours and mine.

Here are the six elements, or principles, to beginning again in a marriage.

1. Acceptance

Accept one another, then, just as Christ accepted you, in order to bring praise to God. (Romans 15:7 NIV)

Without acceptance, the Christian faith as we know it could not exist. Similarly, without acceptance, no marriage could survive the differences sure to surface when two people live together. We are to accept one another the same way God has accepted us—unconditionally.

Many people believe that the majority of husbands and wives have opposite personalities and style. We all know the saying, "opposites attract." In many cases, back in our dating years, we wanted someone who would "balance us out." His outgoing nature helped to "bring her out." Her tendency to plan found a counterpoint in his fun-loving spontaneity. We saw in our "opposites" those traits we wished we had, so it just felt right to be with the other person.

But after marriage—after spending more time together living under the same roof—those little differences don't seem so little anymore. What once seemed so attractive now becomes a point of serious contention, and the things that once felt so endearing become trumpet calls to battle.

If you are to begin again and again in your marriage, you must learn to accept one another, completely and unconditionally. You'll have to look prayerfully at your mate's flaws and idiosyncrasies and realize that since Christ Himself found that person acceptable so should you.

God made us all unique and wildly different from one another. But we are all made in the image of God. When we look at others, especially that person with whom we've made a lifetime commitment, how can we do anything less than accept one another and love one another, just as we promised when we stood at the altar and said, "I do"?

2. Attention

> Now that you have purified yourselves by obeying the truth so that you have sincere love for your brothers, love one another deeply, from the heart. (1 Peter 1:22 NIV)

At first glance, this verse seems like a no-brainer. Of course we have to love one another if we want to restore our marriages and begin again. That should go without saying—but God says it. Why? Because we need to hear it again and again.

We know we're supposed to love one another. The question is, *how* do we do it? What must we actually *do* in order to put action behind the words *I love you?*

It's not as complicated as some people like to make it. In fact, I would simplify it by saying that another way to spell *love* is A-T-T-E-N-T-I-O-N. Nothing signals "love" as clearly as *attention*.

When I was a small child and visitors dropped by the house, I immediately became an acrobat. I would turn somersaults, do handstands, or hang by my feet on a backyard "trapeze." To top it off, I would even sing! I felt eager to get our visitors' attention. I believe many husbands and wives likewise would turn flips, dance around, and belt out songs if they thought it would cause their spouse to focus more on them.

One young man came to me nearly in tears over a relationship that fell apart. He thought he had found the girl of his dreams. They seemed perfectly suited for each another. You never heard his name without hers, and vice versa. Everyone knew they were "an item." But one day she ended it. To put it in his words, she "dumped" him.

"What happened?" I asked.

"I didn't pay attention," he replied. "I got busy doing all kinds of things, and I just quit giving her attention."

We men seem to need "tutoring" on this subject. Somehow giving attention comes a little more naturally to our female counterparts. That's true at least in our family. Jo Beth is an expert at showing attention. So, husbands, let me give a few simple suggestions on giving attention to your wives. Wives, this doesn't mean you're off the hook! I would encourage you to follow these suggestions too:

- Compliment her appearance.
- Buy her a small token of your love (flowers, cards, etc.).
- Go out of your way to thank her for something well done—even everyday chores.
- Call her in the middle of the day, just to talk.
- Speak words of encouragement and praise in front of others.

In countless ways you can give your mate the attention he or she deserves. Be creative. Be spontaneous. But *pay attention* to your partner! You might be amazed at how that kind of attention can help you "begin again and again" in your marriage.

3. Adjustment

And be subject to one another in the fear of Christ. (Ephesians 5:21)

This verse teaches mutual submission. If we want happy marriages, we have to learn to submit to one another. We do this by learning to *adjust* to one another's needs, desires, goals, dreams, and even idiosyncrasies.

Too many people enter marriage convinced they can change their mate. They spot some little flaw in their husband or wife, perhaps a habit, a tendency, a quirk in a lifestyle, or even a harmless hobby. So they threaten, coerce, cajole, or use some other form of pressure to change the undesirable trait or behavior—usually with painful or disastrous results. Instead of adjustment, they get *aggravation!*

Now read this carefully: You *cannot* change your husband or wife. I cannot change Jo Beth and she cannot change me. But we both have learned to give and take, to "adjust" to one another.

Unfortunately, many people go through life unable or unwilling to adjust to others. They become inflexible—selfish-ness of the most destructive kind—and eventually it leads to a break in the relationship. So many marriages doom them-selves from the beginning because one or both partners refuse to submit to the other, to make adjustments to their own schedules and desires and needs.

Fortunately, people can change. I know . . . I just said you can't change your mate, but that doesn't mean that you and your mate can't change! God is in the changing business. He makes all things new[3]—and that goes for our marriages too.

So if you truly want to "begin again" in your marriage, ask the Lord to change you from within. Ask for His forgive-ness for your selfishness and inflexibility. Then ask Him to show you where you need to adjust to your mate.

You know what will happen? He will help you find ways to adjust your own heart and mind to your spouse's needs, desires, and goals. Your husband or wife will see the "new you," and he or she, too, will be changed.

God never wants us to worry about changing other people, just ourselves. Yet in His economy, His changing of us seems to take care of changing that other person!

4. Amnesty

> Be kind to one another, tender-hearted, forgiving each other, just as God in Christ also has forgiven you. (Ephesians 4:32)

Forgiveness is at the heart of Christianity, and it's at the heart of any healthy marriage. It was not long after I said "I do" that I realized forgiveness is an essential ingredient to a happy marriage. That's why I quote this verse to every cou-ple who stands before me at the altar. More than any other verse, this one holds the key to helping a husband and wife work through anything. If every couple put these words into practice, divorce rates would plummet.

Notice I've chosen the word *amnesty* instead of *forgiveness*. The word *amnesty* comes from a Greek word meaning "forgetfulness." While forgiveness means canceling all debts and blame for a wrong committed, amnesty takes this process a step further by declaring the wrongdoer or debtor innocent of all charges. It's as though the offense never happened! Amnesty speaks of a deliberate effort to overlook offenses.

Over the years I've met far too many couples who carry grudges against one another, often for things that happened years, even decades, ago. While marriage is not easy, we can make the road far less bumpy by forgiving our husband's or wife's wrongdoings—over and over again, just as God, through Christ, has forgiven us.

5. Appreciation

Therefore encourage one another and build up one another, just as you also are doing. (1 Thessalonians 5:11)

In this verse Paul gives us the two components of *appreciation:* encouragement and building up. The New Testament word for "encourage" is actually a combination of two words. The first term means to "walk beside" someone in a way that boosts and comforts the person in his journey through life. The other word refers to a "calling" someone receives. In marriage, God has called Jo Beth and me to walk through life, side by side, encouraging and comforting one another wherever our path leads. And you cannot encourage someone in this way without showing appreciation.

We see the second component of appreciation in the word translated "build up." The original Greek term means "to build a house." Paul writes that we are "temples of God" (1 Corinthians 3:16). Therefore, one spouse seeks to build in the other a resplendent temple, not a "fixer upper"! I want Jo Beth to be the grandest house around, and she desires the same for me.

Whenever I show or express my appreciation of her, it's as though I'm adding layer upon layer of valuable stone, raising her higher and higher.

When we encourage and build up our mates, something else happens. Think of what happens when you buy and improve a piece of property. It increases in value; its value *appreciates*.

The same thing happens when we encourage and build up our mates. They appreciate as a person. Our expressions of appreciation actually can help our husbands or wives to improve themselves!

These doses of appreciation should be ministered daily. Hebrews 3:13 says to "encourage one another day after day." We should do this *every time* we recognize something praiseworthy in our mates.

6. Affection

> The husband must fulfill his duty to his wife, and likewise also the wife to her husband. (1 Corinthians 7:3)

When you think of the word *affection*, what comes to mind? Gentle touches? Big, strong "bear hugs"? An arm lovingly placed around the shoulder? We can express affection in many ways, from a simple touch on the hand to the act of sexual intimacy between a husband and wife.

A few years ago I wrote a book titled *Romancing the Home: How to Have a Marriage That Sizzles*. A portion of the book addressed Dr. Willard Harley's survey on the five greatest needs of husbands and wives. That survey revealed that while "sexual fulfillment" is the number one need of husbands from their wives, "affection" is the number one need of wives from their husbands. During this time I preached a sermon on the wife's number one need. To this day, that message (titled "Why Hug?") remains the most requested tape in the history of our media ministry.

The wife's need for affection is so strong that lack of it can lead to an extramarital affair. Most professional counselors agree that women are unfaithful for completely different reasons from men. While unsatisfied sexual needs might send a husband looking elsewhere, a wife can be literally "hugged" into an affair if she is deprived of affection.

Affection provides the "atmosphere" for the relationship. So it's vital that husbands and wives meet one another's needs in this area. A good way to start is with a simple but affectionate hug. After all, a hug can do wonders!

> It's the perfect cure for what ails you. No movable parts; no batteries to wear out; no periodic check ups; low energy consumption; high energy yield; inflation proof; non-taxable; non-polluting; and, of course, fully returnable. Hugging is healthy. It relieves tension, combats depression, reduces stress, and improves blood circulation. It's invigorating, it's rejuvenating, it elevates self-esteem, it generates good will, it has no unpleasant side effects. It is nothing less than a miracle drug.[4]

Affection is not reserved for women. It's a fundamental need of every human. If you don't believe that, take a look at a mother with her young children. There you see touching, hugging, kissing—all acts of affection that reinforce the child's understanding that he or she is special. A mother instinctively knows that her child needs loving attention.

We dads are getting a little better at this. I've always tried to show affection to my boys: a hug, a pat on the back, even a kiss. I still show that affection even though all three are grown with their own children. I love watching them with their kids. They do a great job of showing affection to their wives and their children.

In marriage, sexual intimacy is a vital expression of affection. As our key verse, 1 Corinthians 7:3, commands, "The husband must fulfill his duty to his wife, and likewise also the wife to her husband." God has given this sacred, beautiful gift as a primary means for a couple to share affection with one another.

It is so important, in fact, that Paul tells us that the "wife does not have authority over her own body, but the husband does; and likewise also the husband does not have authority over his own body, but the wife does" (1 Corinthians 7:4). Sex is not only something married couples do for pleasure, it's also a mutual duty for the benefit of each partner. When practiced the way the Bible teaches, sexual intimacy can offset the problem of sexual temptation outside marriage.

Paul encouraged the Corinthians: "Stop depriving one another, except by agreement for a time, so that you may devote yourselves to prayer, and come together again so that Satan will not tempt you because of your lack of self-control" (v. 5). Seen this way, sex between a husband and wife is a *spiritual* responsibility. When practiced according to God's plan, sexual intimacy in marriage contributes to the wholeness and well-being of each partner and enhances their affectionate relationship.

THE LOOK OF A RENEWED MARRIAGE

The State of Your Marriage

During my years as a pastor, I've seen all kinds of marriages. Most can be classified "geographically." For example, there's what I call the "Northern Alaska marriage." Here you'll find extensive frozen tundra—not much emotion, harsh, boring, and lifeless. In this type of marriage, the husband and wife walk around like the living dead from some old horror movie. They pretend to be alive, but the chill in the air quickly snaps at anything living and suffocates it with a biting frost.

There are also "Colorado marriages." Such a relationship goes through seasonal periods of cold and warmth. Winters come when crisis and conflict hit. These seasons are dark, heavy, and filled with icy snow and bitter winds. But the spectacular summers of a Colorado marriage feature clear, crisp air and fabulous views. The problem with this type of marriage is that cold and warm mix to create a sort of "lukewarm" or average marriage. And who likes average? No one wants to be average; that simply means you're the worst of the best and the best of the worst.

Finally, there is the "Hawaii marriage." Ah! This marriage is warm, romantic, beautiful, luxuriant, and growing. The hammock gently sways under the palm trees, the surf pounds the shore, and rainbows fill the sky. Life feels wonderful.

The Challenge

What "state" is your marriage in? If yours is the warm and loving "Hawaiian marriage," you're doing a great job putting God's principles to work in your relationship. If it tends to be more like the "hot and cold" relationship of the "Colorado marriage," then you might need to apply the principles of "beginning again" more consistently. If your marriage has become cold, barren, and lifeless like the tundra of northern Alaska, then it's time for you and your mate to *begin* "beginning again."

The truth is our marriages experience times in all of these "states." That's why it's so important that we follow God's plan for building a marriage that will survive all climates—and move toward more frequent stays in Hawaii! If you apply His six principles for beginning again, you will be well on your way to moving your marriage relationship from the frozen Alaskan tundra to the tropical warmth of the Hawaiian beaches.

REFLECTING ON YOUR RELATIONSHIP

1. What three things would you do differently if you could start your marriage over?
2. Which of the six steps to "beginning again" does your marriage need the most? Explain.
3. Would you consider your marriage warm and loving, hot and cold, or dry and barren? In what ways?
4. Have you hugged your husband or wife today?

A PERSONAL WORD
Thou Shalt Build a Winning Team

In our society many marriages are losing because they haven't put everything in place to build a solid lifestyle that wins. This chapter shows you how to be part of a team that is continuously victorious. Just put the principles into practice, and you will never lose a game!

—E. Y.

Commandment 10

THOU SHALT BUILD
A WINNING TEAM

A pastor greeting members of his congregation as they exited the morning worship service turned toward an approaching couple. He had performed their wedding a few years earlier, so he was a little surprised at their terse "hello" as they walked quickly passed him. After the couple walked away, they whispered to one another, turned, and came back to the pastor.

"Pastor," the man said, "we just want you to know we're getting a divorce, and it's nobody's business but ours."

The minister studied the couple a moment. "That's not right," he said. "Your marriage is *everybody's* business."

OUR MARRIAGES:
THEY'RE THE NATION'S BUSINESS

We live in an age of "personal rights" and "privacy." But we often forget we are part of a larger scheme than our own individual lives and privileges. We are members of a society, and like it or not, your marriage—my marriage—is the *nation's* business.

In Galveston, Texas, not far from Houston, where I live, several wooden piers extend into the Gulf of Mexico. Some serve the fishing industry, while others bear shops and restaurants. The piers stand on pilings sunk into the seafloor. Knock out one of those pilings and the stability of the entire pier suffers. Remove or weaken a number of those pillars and the pier will crash into the waves below, taking everything resting on it into the water.

The crucial question is: How many pilings can you knock out from under a pier and still have it stand?

Individual societies are like those piers, hovering over thundering waves that pound, pressure, and threaten to bring down whole nations and cultures. But God designed marriage to be like those pilings, sunk deep into the foundation of His truth and holding up everything else. In turn, those marriages serve as pilings for families—people learn to function as stable and productive citizens when they come from solid homes. In the home we can learn self-discipline, respect, and responsibility. As noted by Francis Fukuyama, professor of international political economics at John Hopkins University,

> "Civil society"—a complex welter of intermediate institutions, including businesses, voluntary associations, educational institutions, clubs, unions, media, charities, and churches— builds, in turn, on the family, the primary instrument by which people are socialized into their culture and given the skills that allow them to live in broader society and through which the values and knowledge of that society are transmitted across the generations.[1]

As marriages grow weaker, families grow weaker, and all society suffers as a result. That pastor rightly told the couple their divorce was everybody's business. How many marriages can be knocked from under the "pier" of America and the nation still stand?

OUR MARRIAGES:
THEY'RE OUR CHILDREN'S BUSINESS

Our marriages are certainly our *children's* business. Children are like seismographs. The slightest tremor in the relationship between their mother and father registers on their psyche.

The parents' relationship sets in motion entire destinies, since the way we love our children, nurture them, and make them feel secure affects their future marriages and families. George Gallup's research, for example, shows that daughters of single parents have a *164 percent* greater chance of having a child out of wedlock, a *111 percent* higher rate of teen motherhood, and are *92 percent* more likely to divorce than girls reared by married parents.[2] As noted in chapter 6 (see page 130), children raised in fatherless homes are more likely to engage in criminal behavior as teens or adults.

Beyond all doubt, our marriages are our children's business.

OUR MARRIAGES: THEY'RE GOD'S BUSINESS

Our marriages are also *God's* business. As we saw in a previous chapter, because God loves, He communicates with those He loves—namely, us.

Good communicators use a common frame of reference to connect with their audiences. A person seeking to give a message to another will consider where their lives and experiences overlap and begin at that common point. That's why God frequently talks to us in domestic terms. For example, the Bible says, "As a father has compassion on his children, so the LORD has compassion on those who fear Him" (Psalm 103:13). Again, God says through Isaiah, "As one whom his mother comforts, so I will comfort you" (Isaiah 66:13).

How can an individual sense the meaning of a father's loving compassion if no dad has blessed that person's life, whether because of divorce, separation, or death? What does maternal comfort signify to a man or woman deprived of a mom in the developmental years? God, like a loving father, cares about His children; that includes caring about our welfare in a marriage covenant affirmed before Him as well as witnesses.

It's also God's business because He uses our marriage to teach others about their relationship with Christ. Husbands, Paul wrote, are to love their wives in the same way that Christ loved the church—to the point of their own sacrifice, if necessary (Ephesians 5:25). When a husband doesn't love his wife as described here, the verse and its principle lose impact and even meaning. *When a marriage breaks up, the best theological school God designed ceases to function.*

It is sheer arrogance to say, "Our marriage is no one else's business." In fact, it is the business of God, the children involved, and the nation itself.

A DYNAMIC RELATIONSHIP

Because marriage is "everybody's business," it's essential that every husband and wife develop a dynamic relationship.

As we've considered these commandments to build healthy marriages, we've received some very practical insights. This tenth and final commandment cradles the previous nine, because if our marriages are going to grow strong through the years, both partners must work together—and that means teamwork! Therefore, *thou shalt build a winning team.*

A team exists when a group of two or more individuals works toward the same goal or objective. Members of the team may not share the same ideas about how to achieve their shared objective, but they all keep the same ultimate goals in mind.

God's plan for marriage included teamwork from the very

beginning. So let's see what it takes to build a winning husband-wife team.

TEAMWORK IN THE GARDEN

At the dawn of creation, God said of His plans for Adam, "It is not good for the man to be alone; I will make him a *helper* suitable for him" (Genesis 2:18, emphasis added).

Adam had looked all around the beautiful paradise God had created for him, and he detected something intriguing: Every creature had its own partner. All the mammals, birds, reptiles, and fish had counterparts that looked much like them, yet with crucial differences. Adam noticed, however, that he had no such counterpart—and God took it upon Himself to make sure the man received the perfect teammate. He created a woman from the rib of the man, and Adam immediately rejoiced in his new partner: "This is now bone of my bones, and flesh of my flesh; she shall be called Woman, because she was taken out of Man." God intended the new couple to form such a close-knit team that He called them "one flesh" (vv. 23–24).

King Solomon later espoused the crucial value of teamwork when he wrote, "Two are better than one, because they have a good return for their work: If one falls down, his friend can help him up. But pity the man who falls and has no one to help him up! Also, if two lie down together, they will keep warm. But how can one keep warm alone?" (Ecclesiastes 4:9–11 NIV).

The Ecclesiastes passage looks like a promotion for the institution of marriage. God clearly intended for marriage to be a team effort. One biblical couple, in particular, perfectly supports such a conclusion.

A NEW TESTAMENT TEAM

The marriage of Priscilla and Aquila, two faithful servants of Christ, shows the widespread impact of a dynamic husband-wife team. The fact that one is never mentioned in the Bible without the other speaks of the vitality of their marriage.

We know little about them. They had lived in Rome but had to leave when the Emperor Claudius expelled the Jews. Like Paul, they became tent makers. In fact, this is how Paul met them in Corinth. Since the city provided few places for travelers to lodge, Paul stayed with Priscilla and Aquila (Acts 18:1–3). So long as Paul remained in a community, he made it his habit to make tents during the week and teach each Sabbath in the synagogue. As devout Jews, Priscilla and Aquila attended the services. When Silas and Timothy arrived in Corinth after preaching in Macedonia, Paul was able to spend all his time teaching.

In Paul's epistle to the Romans, we learn that Priscilla and Aquila actually saved Paul's life, at great risk to their own (16:3–4). The local church met in the house of this husband and wife team (v. 5). Paul spoke with obvious affection for these two, even insisting that the Gentile churches owed them thanks. Paul also passed a greeting from Aquila and Priscilla to the Christians in Corinth and instructed the young pastor Timothy to pass along a greeting to them in Ephesus (1 Corinthians 16:19; 2 Timothy 4:19).

Aquila and Priscilla—two simple, blue-collar workers won to Christ by the apostle Paul—give us a great picture of marital teamwork. Their united efforts well qualify them as unsung heroes of the Christian faith. They traveled with Paul, planted a church, held worship services in their home, and even saved the life of the man who would become one of the most important figures in the history of Christianity.

Priscilla and Aquila became important not only to individuals but to their whole community as well. Wherever they lived, this godly couple made their house a church. Everyone knew they could find light, hope, and love in their home.

But what if there had been no Priscilla and Aquila? What

if this team had broken apart? Their marriage and its enormous impact was certainly "everybody's business." This couple helped saved Paul's life, and Paul took the gospel to the Gentile world. Through the centuries, the Good News spread throughout Europe and eventually came to the shores of our own nation. So you see, Priscilla and Aquila's marriage is *"our business"* even today!

These two first-century Christians made up a winning team—and I believe God wants to build equally powerful teams today. So let's look at what it takes to build a Priscilla-and-Aquila kind of marriage.

COMPONENTS FOR WINNING TEAMS

Deciding to Build

Proverbs 24:3–4 tells us, "By wisdom a house [or a marriage] is built, and by understanding it is established; and by knowledge the rooms are filled with all precious and pleasant riches." The word *built* is an action verb, whether the context is home, construction, or marriage.

We must *decide* to build a winning team. If we commit ourselves to building a winning team, God can give us the wisdom, the understanding, and the knowledge required for success.

Building a Winning Team

Have you ever wondered what it takes to build a winner? Consider, for example, what it takes to build a winning college football team. Several key components go into developing a champion on the gridiron.

1. *A competent architect.* Every winning college team has an "architect" for the program. It takes a composite of the top leadership—the university chancellor, president, board of trustees, and athletic director. This group lays

out the parameters of the school's sports activities and provides the funding. If this group of individuals remains totally committed to building a winner, the team is on its way to a successful program.

2. *A knowledgeable coach.* This individual must be able to get along with the university administration, recruit players, build and lead a staff, operate within a budget, and motivate talented young players. Knute Rockne, legendary coach at the University of Notre Dame, was such a man. When he died in an airplane crash, a newspaper editorialized, "Anyone who can fire the manhood of others as he did is in every way admirable."

3. *Talented players.* Every winning team has a wealth of gifted athletes, diverse talent harnessed together into one squad. A coaching staff can't build a team of 185-pound running backs only, or build a winner with nothing but 300-pound linemen. The right mix of size and skill is vital. But all players must have one thing in common: They must buy into the coaching staff's program. They have to believe in what the head coach and his coaching staff have taught them.

4. *The intangibles.* Winning college football programs master what we would call "the intangibles." These teams create an atmosphere of discipline and togetherness, two vital factors in winning. Vince Lombardi, who was one of pro football's best coaches, said, "There is something good in men that really yearns for discipline." Legendary University of Alabama coach Bear Bryant once said of his success, "I'm just a simple plow hand from Arkansas, but I have learned over the years how to hold a team together. How to lift some men up, how to calm others down, until finally they've got one heartbeat, together, a team." Togetherness—*many hearts working as one*—that's essential for a winning team.

5. *Fan support.* In 2002, the Houston Texans won their opening game against the Dallas Cowboys, becoming the first pro football team in forty-one years to win their debut as an expansion team. Bob McNair, owner of the Texans, built Reliant Stadium to be open or closed for weather reasons, but the noise cascading onto the field is another benefit of the closed stadium. The loud fans cheered their new team to a stunning upset. The expansion Texans upset the established and heavily favored Cowboys, so I'd say the home field advantage helped!

All these ingredients must go into the mix of a winning football team. When they all come together, a winner eventually emerges; it's only a matter of time. I believe similar principles can be applied to building a winning team in marriage.

COMPONENTS FOR A WINNING MARRIAGE TEAM

Just as a football team needs an architect, a coach, players, the intangibles, and fan support in order to win, so a winning marriage must put all the right pieces in place.

1. The Eternal Architect

Building a winning college football team requires a commitment to success, starting at the very top. The same is true of building a winning marriage. We have an Architect who wants to see us succeed in our marriages even more than we do.

The prophet Malachi lived in an era when his people increasingly turned to divorce as a "solution" for their marital ills. Sound familiar? This, he knew, greatly displeased the Lord, for God intended husbands and wives to function as a single unit. "Has not the LORD made them one?" the prophet asked. "In flesh and spirit they are his. . . . So guard yourself in your spirit, and do not break faith with the wife of your youth. 'I hate divorce,' says the LORD God of Israel. . . . So guard yourself in your spirit, and do not break faith" (Malachi 2:15–16 NIV).

Our heavenly Father designed marriage to be a perfect union. While the arrival of sin has damaged that union, we still can build a winning team—*if* we follow the Architect's instructions. He loves us and wants married couples to reflect His love, both to one another and to those around them. He graciously gives us more than enough wisdom, understanding, and knowledge to create a winning marriage team. But more than that, He sent us the ultimate gift of love in our "Head Coach," Jesus Christ.

2. The Right Coach

A college administration that wants to build a winning football team looks for a coach who not only *tells* the players what it takes to win but *shows* them by his own actions. It should come as no surprise that our Head Coach for a winning marriage team is Jesus Christ. If a husband and wife have committed themselves individually to Christ, He is in their lives personally—and He has the "playbook."

Our earlier verse in Proverbs 24 describes what Jesus brings to the marriage team: "By wisdom a house is built, and by understanding it is established" (v. 3). Let's look at the wisdom and understanding our Coach brings to a marriage team.

The Hebrew word for *wisdom* in Proverbs refers to "practical smarts." In other words, we have competence and confidence as we face life's realities. God's wisdom is not just theoretical stuff, but the sense of knowing how to do specific things. God means for His principles to be understood and applied to our everyday lives.

It's no surprise, then, when Paul refers to Jesus as the "wisdom from God" (1 Corinthians 1:30). Christ is the practical demonstration of God's wisdom. He's God's wisdom with hands and feet.

"All the treasures of wisdom and knowledge" are in Jesus Christ (Colossians 2:3). Think of it this way: When Bear Bryant walked onto a football field, he carried in his head all the "treasures of wisdom and knowledge" of football strategy that made him one of the greatest, most successful coaches in history. His mere presence generated confidence in his team and assistant coaches. They trusted his football wisdom.

The staggering reality is that a husband and wife who have individually invited Christ into their lives "have the mind of Christ" (1 Corinthians 2:16). All the treasures of Christ's mind are now in the spirit of the person in whom He dwells. The issue is accessing what we already have and putting it to practical use.

How do we access the mind of our "coach" in our marriage? The most successful young men who played for Coach Bryant sought to know their leader as closely as possible. They tried to think like the great coach and imagine how he would respond in a given situation. Similarly, the more we walk in intimacy with Jesus Christ, the more the treasures of His wisdom and knowledge become ours. He says this closeness with Him must be so tight it is like a branch attached to a vine (see John 15). Jesus even makes the shocking claim that "if you abide in Me, and My words abide in you, ask whatever you wish, and it will be done for you" (John 15:7).

What a tremendous promise! If Jesus lives in us and we live in Him, then we will know how He thinks and what He wants, and therefore will ask for what He desires. We will pray the perfect will of God, and that's what we will get!

The key to a husband and wife applying the wisdom of the "coach" to their marriage is, first, to receive Christ; and, second, to become intimate with Him through the continual study of His Word, prayer, and worship. The more such wisdom prevails in a marriage, the more the relationship grows.

Jesus also brings the understanding essential for building

a winning marriage team. Wisdom, says Proverbs 24:3, builds the house, but "understanding" establishes it. In other words, it is *understanding* that brings stability to the marriage. *Wisdom* is the condition, or state, and *understanding* is its practical outcome.

When Jesus was twelve years old, He accompanied His parents to Jerusalem, where He dialogued with the leaders of the temple. They were "amazed at His understanding and His answers," reported Luke (2:47). The Greek word for *understanding* comes from a term meaning "to put things together mentally." Jesus had the ability to see the big picture, to see how everything fit into place. If He had been a coach diagramming plays, all His "X's" and O's" would have worked out perfectly on the field—every time!

One of the hit television situation comedies is *Frasier.* The program features two brothers, both psychiatrists. The humor is in the depiction of both as "brainy" but having almost no common sense. Frasier can quote Freud at length, but has been divorced three times. He and his brother, Niles, can sing operas by heart, but hardly know how to communicate effectively with common people. They see ethereal issues, but miss the most glaring occurrences.

But the husband and wife team who follow Jesus Christ as their marriage "Coach" will gain the understanding to resist the destructive tugs inevitable in a fallen world such as ours.

3. The Players

Some coaches are better than others at getting the best out of their players. Not only do winning coaches find talented players for their programs, they also properly develop these athletes so they perform to their full potential. Some coaches seem to have the uncanny ability to find talented yet overlooked players and turn them into superstars.

God has recruited us as players for His kingdom's purposes. When we allow Jesus Christ to be our Coach, He can take our most ordinary talents and abilities and do extraordinary things with them. Without Christ on our side, we can do nothing. But with Christ on our side, we have all the talent we need to build a winning marriage team.

Like a lot of players, though, we need pep talks. We need to hear we can do it, even when we're two touchdown underdogs! A good coach never lets his team think like a loser. He never allows the word "can't" to become part of his players' vocabulary. Neither will our Lord.

We tend to follow the example of Moses, who came up with every excuse in the book when God commissioned him to lead the people of Israel out of captivity. While Moses said, "Who am I that You should ask me to do this?" we tend to say, "I've tried everything for our marriage, what more can I do?" While Moses said, "I'm not a great speaker," we sometimes complain, "My spouse and I don't communicate very well." While Moses said, "I don't have the strength it takes to do such a task," we say, "I don't think I have the emotional energy to keep working on this marriage."

And what is God's answer? "You *can* do it, because *I'm* going with you!" Or as the apostle Paul put it, "I can do all things through Him who strengthens me" (Philippians 4:13). Because you and your mate have been chosen by Him, the two of you have all the talent you need to become a winning team. In fact, with the Lord working in us, making the necessary changes and adjustments from the inside, there is nothing we *can't* do!

4. The Intangibles

Just as every winning football team needs to develop the intangibles, the little things that make for a winner, so does every winning marriage. So what intangibles can help a marriage build a winning tradition? Let me start with what I consider to be the most important.

The first intangible is *goal setting*. A couple has to set long-term goals as well as short-term goals. When I've asked couples about their goals in marriage, I've heard some very telling answers. "Right now," some have told me, "we're just working to hang in there and stay together." As a short-term goal, that's not bad; but in order to build a winning marriage team, we need long-term goals.

Perhaps the one indispensable long-term goal in marriage is to become the kind of lovers who will love one another as God has loved us, till death do us part. Does that sound like an irrational, unconditional, supernatural love, a love that gives and gives and gives some more? I suppose it does. But nothing else will suffice.

The second intangible is *commitment*. Football teams armed with a brilliant architect, a great coach, and talented players still won't accomplish much without a commitment to winning. The same is true of our marriages. Commitment means that you stick with the program, even in down years. Commitment means that you constantly search for better ways to do what needs to be done. Commitment means that you develop a vision for the future and that you persevere in order to bring that vision to fruition.

Commitment demands perseverance because no winning program enjoys an unbroken record of sustained success. No team goes unbeaten year after year, decade after decade. Our marriage teams need to develop the kind of perseverance described by the writer of Hebrews:

> You need to persevere so that when you have done the will of God, you will receive what he has promised. For in just a very little while, "He who is coming will come and will not delay. But my righteous one will live by faith. And if he shrinks back, I will not be pleased with him." But we are not of those who

shrink back and are destroyed, but of those who believe and are saved. (10:36–39 NIV)

Do you want to be part of a winning team in marriage? Then you must make the kind of commitment that leads to perseverance.

The third intangible is *discipline*. It takes discipline to build a winning marriage team. To run the race of life, said Paul, "I discipline my body" (1 Corinthians 9:27). The idea behind the Greek word Paul uses is the subduing or controlling of passions. If you train, you discipline.

It's important in marriage to build disciplines governing how the couple makes decisions, how the husband and wife handle their children in unity, how they structure and spend the family budget, how they resolve conflicts, as well as disciplines in many other areas. And the children of such a marriage learn the importance of self-control through the modeling of their parents.

The fourth intangible is *togetherness*. Ecclesiastes points out the practical value of togetherness. Read again Ecclesiastes 4:9–11 and note the outcome of working together.

First, a husband and wife working together will "have a good return for their labor" (v. 9). Literally, "return" means "compensation." Husbands and wives functioning as a unit in decision making have a greater "payoff" in terms of decisions that are well considered and solid.

Second, in a marriage in which the husband and wife are working together, there is constant encouragement for each other. If one falls, the other is there to lift up the spouse. If a husband slides into self-doubt and a loss of confidence, the wife, in such a "together" relationship, will be sensitive to her mate's plight and encourage him. If the wife concludes she is a failure, her "teammate" offers reassurance. Together, the husband and wife are continually building up one another.

Third, in a marriage characterized by togetherness, the partners "warm" each other. The Hebrew word for "warm" in this passage means, among other things, "inflamed." This is much more than providing physical warmth. A "together" marriage offers passion, enthusiasm, and mutual encouragement. The husband and wife look for opportunities to pat the other on the back and recognize achievements and successes.

According to verse 12, there is a fourth benefit of a together marriage: strength. "And if one can overpower him who is alone, two can resist him. A cord of three strands is not quickly torn apart." Stress from the outside world exerts a pull on spouses, threatening to yank them apart. Money, jobs, temptations, gender roles, and expectations all are part of this force pulling at the togetherness of a husband and wife. It requires a power greater than all these at the core of the marriage to exert a magnetic force so strong it cannot be overwhelmed.

That is what happens when a couple puts God at the center of their relationship. His strength at the center of the marriage is so great the relationship cannot be pulled apart, no matter how great the stress.

5. Fan Support

"Fan support" is as much a necessity for a winning marriage team as for an athletic team. In marriage, that support comes from the encouragement of family, friends, children, coworkers, and the church family.

Hebrews 12 describes a "great cloud of witnesses" that cheers on God's people in their "race" in this fallen world (v. 1). These witnesses encourage us to lay aside the hindrances that keep us from running a victorious race and to run with endurance. So in a marriage, "fans" can provide encouragement to a husband and wife in their winning relationship. That means it's important for a couple to choose friends who will provide such positive support.

While in Paris years ago, I remember seeing the majestic Cathedral of Notre Dame. The structure receives external support from its famous "flying buttresses." These huge stone props exert external force on the cathedral and brace it against collapse. So in a marriage, support from the "outside" intensifies the unity inside.

That brings us back to Priscilla and Aquila and their strong marriage. They received "external" support in the person of the apostle Paul and the Christians who gathered in their house as the church. Whether in Corinth, Ephesus, or Rome, they received strength and encouragement in both their individual lives and in their marital relationship through their fellowship with the followers of Jesus.

Husbands and wives today must have a similar kind of fan base to build a winning marriage team. It requires the teachers who minister God's Word, along with fellow believers who lead the cheers. All this comes to spouses through weekly church assemblies and also through small groups, classes, and other elements of a thriving church.

THE ROLE OF
DETERMINATION AND COMMITMENT

All the support in the world will come to nothing without the strong determination and a passionate commitment on the part of a husband and wife to develop a winning marriage team.

Kathleen Kauth walked through a hotel lobby in Portland, Oregon, and glanced at a television picture. Chills coursed through her body. She had just landed on a stopover after a grueling flight from China, where she had played with the U.S. Women's Hockey Team.

The date was September 11, 2001.

Kathleen could not take her eyes off the screen's horrifying images of the burning towers of New York's World Trade

Center. What especially froze her heart was the knowledge that her father, Donald, worked as a bank analyst in one of the towers. All that day she waited anxiously for a phone call from her dad that never came. He died in the attack.

But just fifteen days after the loss of her father, Kathleen inspired her team with her commitment. She skated back on the ice, determined to win a spot on the U.S. Olympic Team. "That's what my dad would have wanted," she told her friends. Her teammates agreed.

"I think this was the first step in really bringing this team together," forward Krissy Wendell said. "It really bonded this team."

"We need each other and to be strong for each other," said another. "We need each other more than ever now."[3]

Kathleen's example reveals a dynamic cycle. Her passion resulted in personal commitment demonstrated by a determination that inspired passion, commitment, and determination in her teammates. Any team can have the greatest of coaches and strategies and the most enthusiastic of fans. But without passion, commitment, and determination, that team will lose.

WORKING TOGETHER TO WIN

Few would argue that Vince Lombardi, famed coach of football's Green Bay Packers, set the standard for world championship teams. The coveted Super Bowl trophy bears his name. Without a doubt, Lombardi knew how to win. He once said, "Teamwork is what the Green Bay Packers were all about. They didn't do it for individual glory. They did it because they loved one another."[4] The Hall of Fame coach knew that winning was all about "the team."

I think Priscilla and Aquila would have agreed with Lombardi's take on teamwork. They would have smiled to hear him say, "People who work together will win, whether it be against complex football defenses, or the problems of modern society."[5] I think they would have nodded their heads, grabbed each other's hands, looked into one another's eyes, and said in unison, "That's true, Coach. But it's just as true in marriage."

Do you want to win in marriage? God created every marriage to be a winning team. If you wisely apply His principles for success to your own marriage, then you can be a blessing not merely to one another but to the world around you.

Just like Priscilla and Aquila.

REFLECTING ON YOUR RELATIONSHIP

1. If your marriage were indeed a college football team, where would it be ranked?

   ❏ We're in the top five, vying for the championship.
   ❏ We're in the top ten, thrown for a loss once in a while, but we're a winning team.
   ❏ We win some, we lose some, but we could be a lot better.
   ❏ We're losing more than we win; we don't let the Coach lead us in the day-to-day part of our marriage.

2. In what areas does your mate need some "coaching"? What about you?
3. How do your family and friends provide "fan support" for your marriage?
4. What is the greatest strength of your marriage team?

A FINAL WORD

Well, I hope I accomplished my two goals with this book. My goals were to *convince* you that you can have a great marriage—and to *challenge* you to do whatever it takes to achieve a great marriage.

As I was trying to think of a marriage that might sum up the kind of love, fun, affection, and commitment that results from putting into practice these ten marriage principles, I kept coming back to a story I heard years ago. It's about a couple I'll call Bob and Sarah.

They had been married for fifty years. Bob and Sarah were so much in love—they touched, they laughed, they teased, and they played. From the early days of their union, they had played a crazy little game that no one understood. They would write down a funny little word on a piece of paper and hide it in different places around the house. The word was "SHMILY."

There were times Sarah would look in the sugar bowl, and there it was: SHMILY. Bob would get out of the shower and see it written across the steamed up mirror: SHMILY. Once Ann unrolled a whole roll of toilet paper and wrote it on the last sheet: SHMILY.

They played this game their entire married life. Their children knew about the game, but no one knew what SHMILY meant. They weren't even sure how to pronounce it!

Not long after their fifty-second wedding anniversary, doctors diagnosed Sarah with cancer. She battled the disease for nearly ten years. Everyone marveled as they watched this couple stand together through it all. And all the while they continued their SHMILY game. Then, one day, Sarah died.

The funeral provided a glorious time for celebrating her wonderful life, but it was tinged with sadness. The children, the grandchildren, and by now even great-grandchildren watched Bob as he said good-bye to his beloved wife, his teammate for more than sixty years.

Silence reigned on the drive to the cemetery. When they arrived at the graveside, they all noticed the big pink ribbon on the casket—and there it was, in big letters on the ribbon: SHMILY! They watched as he walked up to the casket and in a soft, deep voice began to sing to her. As one, the family held hands and began to cry.

Most everyone had quietly moved away so he could have a moment alone. But one of his granddaughters, a young teenager, stayed behind. She reached out and took hold of his hand.

"Grandpa," she said, "tell me, what does SHMILY mean?"

Bob looked into her eyes and with a tender smile, replied, "SHMILY stands for See How Much I Love You."

How much should we love our spouse? As much as Christ loves the church. Recall and practice the command of Ephesians 5:25–27: "Love your [spouse], just as Christ also loved the church and gave Himself up for her, so that He might sanctify her, having cleansed her by the washing of water with the word, that He might present to Himself the church in all her glory, having no spot or wrinkle or any such thing; but that she would be holy and blameless."

SUGGESTED READING

Collins, Gary R. *Family Shock.* Wheaton, Ill.: Tyndale, 1995.

Hendricks, Howard and Jeanne Hendricks, eds. *Husbands and Wives.* Colorado Springs: Chariot Victor, 1989.

Jenkins, Jerry B. *Loving Your Marriage Enough to Protect It.* Chicago: Moody, 1993.

Lawson, Steven J. *The Legacy: What Every Father Wants to Leave His Child.* Sisters, Oreg.: Multnomah, 1998.

Lowery, Fred. *Covenant Marriage: Staying Together for Life.* West Monroe, La.: Howard, 2002.

Perkins, Bill. *Fatal Attractions.* Eugene, Oreg.: Harvest House, 1991.

Rainey, Dennis. *One Home at a Time.* Colorado Springs: Focus on the Family, 1997.

Rainey, Dennis and Barbara Rainey. *Building Your Mate's Self-Esteem.* Nashville: Nelson, 1995.

Swindoll, Charles R. *Strike the Original Match.* Wheaton, Ill.: Tyndale, 1990.

Thomas, Gary. *Sacred Marriage.* Grand Rapids: Zondervan, 2000.

Wright, H. Norman. *Romancing Your Marriage.* Ventura, Calif.: Regal, 1987.

Young, Ben and Samuel Adams. *The One: A Realistic Guide for Choosing Your Soul Mate.* Nashville: Nelson, 2001.

NOTES

Commandment 1: Thou Shalt Not Be a Selfish Pig

1. Willard F. Harley Jr., "How the Co-dependency Movement Is Ruining Marriages," article on the Internet at www.marriagebuilders.com/graphic/mbi8110_cod.html. Accessed on 5 December 2002.
2. *The 365 Stupidest Things Ever Said* calendar, Tuesday, October 24, 2000, Workman Publishing.
3. John Piper, *Desiring God*, 10th Anniversary ed. (Sisters, Oreg.: Multnomah, 1996), 187.

Commandment 2: Thou Shalt Cut the Apron Strings

1. Genesis 2:24; Matthew 19:5; Mark 10:7–8; 1 Corinthians 6:16; Ephesians 5:31.
2. Amy Dickinson, "Take a Pass on the Postnup," *Time,* 23 July 2001, 73.

Commandment 3: Thou Shalt Continually Communicate

1. Eileen Silva Kindig, "Squeezed for Time?" *Marriage Partnership,* summer 1998, 42.
2. Stephen Seplow and Jonathan Storm, "Remote Control: 50 Years of TV Time," *Philadelphia Inquirer,* 30 November 1997, B6.
3. "A.C.M.E. History and Basic Principles," as cited on the Internet at http://www.bettermarriages.org/publications/history.html. Accessed on 31 January 2003.
4. For example, John Powell notes five levels of communication between two people. See his work cited in Jack and Carole Mayhall, *Marriage Takes More than Love* (Colorado Springs: NavPress, 1978), 88.

5. Adapted from Patricia McGerr, "Johnny Lingo's Eight-Cow Wife," *Reader's Digest,* February 1988, 138–41. Originally published in *Woman's Day,* November 1965.

6. Ibid., 141.

Commandment 4: Thou Shalt Make Conflict Thy Ally

1. Loren Stein, "Building Bliss" at http://www.blueprintforhealth.com/topic/brmarriage. Accessed in 31 January, 2003. Stein reviews findings in John Gottman, *Seven Principles to Making Marriage Work* (New York: Three Rivers Press, 2000).

Commandment 5: Thou Shalt Avoid the Quicksand of Debt

1. Russel D. Crossan, presentation at Focus on the Family Physicians Conference, November 1998, Clearwater, Florida.

2. "J. Paul Getty Dead at 83," *New York Times,* 6 June 1976.

3. See George M. Bowman, *How to Succeed with Your Money* (Chicago: Moody, 1960); and George Fooshee, *You Can Be Financially Free* (Old Tappan, N.J.: Revell, 1976).

4. James Patterson and Peter Kim, *The Day America Told the Truth* (New York: Prentice Hall, 1991), 66.

5. Ed Young, *Fatal Distractions* (Nashville: Thomas Nelson, 2000).

6. Luke 19:9.

Commandment 6: Thou Shalt Flee Sexual Temptation—
Online and Otherwise

1. The account of David and Bathsheba and the resulting consequences is found in 2 Samuel 11–12.

2. The story is found in Genesis 39.

3. "Forecast 2000," report of the Gallup Organization, Princeton, N.J.; as cited in William J. Bennett, *Index of Leading Cultural Indicators* (Washington: Empower America, 2001), 56.

4. Ibid., 59.

5. Ibid., 54.

6. Lisa Beamer, "It's the Day's Very Darkness That Lights Our Path," *Houston Chronicle,* 10 March 2002, 3c–5c.

7. I heard about Lewis's story years ago and I do not remember the source.

Commandment 8: Thou Shalt Keep the Home Fires Burning

1. Robert Browning, "Rabbi Ben Ezra," *Dramatis Personae* (London: Chapman & Hall 1864), n.p.

2. Annette P. Bowen, *Focus on the Family,* February 1989, 8.

3. Kay Kuzma, "Celebrating Marriage," *Family Life Today,* May–June 1986, 14.

4. Bill and Nancie Carmichael and Dr. Timothy Boyd, "Paving the Way to Intimacy," *Virtue,* March/April 1988, 16.

5. Kenneth S. Kantzer, "The Freedom of Jealousy," *Christianity Today*, 21 October 1988, 11.

6. Nathaniel Branden, "Advice That Could Save Your Marriage," *Reader's Digest*, October 1985, 27.

7. Elizabeth Cody Newenhuyse, "Train Up a . . . Spouse?" *Today's Christian Woman*, March/April 1989, 32.

Commandment 9: Thou Shalt Begin Again and Again

1. T. L. Haines and L. W. Yaggy, *The Royal Path of Life* (Philadelphia: Eastern Publishing, 1880), n.p.

2. Adapted from David Ferguson and Don McMinn, *Top 10 Intimacy Needs*, a booklet published by Intimacy Press for the Center of Marriage and Family Intimacy, Austin, Texas, pages 23–35.

3. See 2 Corinthians 5:17.

4. "The Hug"; source unknown.

Commandment 10: Thou Shalt Build a Winning Team

1. Francis Fukuyama, *Trust: The Social Virtues and the Creation of Prosperity* (New York: Simon & Schuster, 1995), 5.

2. As cited in William Bennett, *Index of Leading Cultural Indicators* (Washington: Empower America, 2001), 55.

3. Damian Cristodero, "Determination After Tragedy Bonds Team," *St. Petersburg Times*, 21 October 2001, 7C.

4. As cited on the Internet at http://www.vincelombardi.com/quotes/teamwork.html. Accessed on 17 January 2003.

5. Ibid.

SINCE 1894, Moody Publishers has been dedicated to equip and motivate people to advance the cause of Christ by publishing evangelical Christian literature and other media for all ages, around the world. Because we are a ministry of the Moody Bible Institute of Chicago, a portion of the proceeds from the sale of this book go to train the next generation of Christian leaders.

If we may serve you in any way in your spiritual journey toward understanding Christ and the Christian life, please contact us at www.moodypublishers.com.

"All Scripture is God-breathed and is useful for teaching, rebuking, correcting and training in righteousness, so that the man of God may be thoroughly equipped for every good work."
—2 TIMOTHY 3:16, 17

MOODY
PUBLISHERS

THE NAME YOU CAN TRUST®

THE 10 COMMANDMENTS OF MARRIAGE TEAM

ACQUIRING EDITOR
Mark Tobey

COPY EDITOR
Jim Vincent

BACK COVER COPY
The Smartt Guys

COVER DESIGN
The Smartt Guys

COVER PHOTO
Britt Erlanson/The Image Bank

INTERIOR DESIGN
Ragont Design

PRINTING AND BINDING
Quebecor World Book Services

The typeface for the text of this book is
New Aster

New moms and dads always have the same reaction: "I had no idea it would be this hard!"

ISBN: 0-8024-3147-X

But you can make it a little easier—and a lot more rewarding — simply by following
The Ten Commandments of Parenting..

Relax! God doesn't expect you to be a perfect parent. And He certainly understands that children can be difficult to manage. This is why He didn't leave you alone to figure out parenting on your own. He has provided principles for raising great kids in the pages of His Word.

If your kids are headed in the wrong direction, this could be the turning point you've been praying for. And if you're a brand new parent, you'll thank God for this chance to build your child's character on solid ground.

Post these 10 commandments in your home. Hide them in your heart. And discover just how wonderful it feels to be the best parent you can be.

MOODY
PUBLISHERS
THE NAME YOU CAN TRUST.

1-800-678-6928 www.MoodyPublishers.org